Models of learning – tools for teaching

Bruce Joyce, Emily Calhoun and David Hopkins

Open University Press
Buckingham · Philadelphia

Open University Press
Celtic Court
22 Ballmoor
Buckingham
MK18 1XW

email: enquiries@openup.co.uk
world wide web: http://www.openup.co.uk

and
325 Chestnut Street
Philadelphia, PA 19106, USA

First Published 1997
Reprinted 1999

A catalogue record of this book is available from the British Library

ISBN 0 335 19990 9

Library of Congress Cataloging-in-Publication Data
Joyce, Bruce R.
    Models of learning : tools for teaching / Bruce Joyce, Emily Calhoun,
    David Hopkins.
        p.   cm.
    Includes bibliographical references and index.
    ISBN 0-335-19990-9
    1. Teaching.   2. Learning.   I. Calhoun, Emily.   II. Hopkins,
    David, 1949–   .   III. Title.
    LB1025.3.J69   1997
    371.1'02–dc21   97–11356
                                                                  CIP

Copy-editing, design and typesetting by The Running Head Limited, London
    and Cambridge
Printed in Great Britain by Redwood Books, Trowbridge

To the memory of Lawrence Stenhouse

One of the great seekers of knowledge about teaching
and curriculum, as well as a tireless campaigner for the
empowerment of pupils, teachers and schools

Contents

Scenarios

SCENARIO I: CHILDREN STUDYING HOW THEIR LANGUAGE WORKS

Judith's 5-year-olds at Hempshill Hall primary school are working on building their reading vocabularies. They are also beginning their study of phonics by analysing the structures (spelling) of words that are in their listening, speaking and reading vocabularies.

The children are seated on the floor, facing a poster that features a teddy bear in the countryside. The poster is mounted in the middle of a large blank sheet of paper. Judith says, 'We're going to get some of the words for this week's reading vocabulary by shaking words out of this picture. I want you to look at the picture carefully and then, when I call on you, come up and point to something in the picture and say what it is. Then I'll write the word and draw a line from the thing in the picture to the word. We'll start learning to read the words as we go along.'

The children study the picture. After a while, Judith asks them if they have found something they'd like to share. All the hands go up, and Judith calls on Jessica.

Jessica reaches up, points and says 'That's a ladder.' Judith draws a line from the ladder and writes the word *ladder*, saying the letters as she does so. She then spells *ladder* again, while the children watch and listen.

'Now, I'll spell it again, and you say each letter after me.' She does, and then asks another child for a word.

'Sit' says Brian, and points to the teddy bear. 'The bear's sitting.'

Judith draws a line from the bear and writes, *The bear's sitting*. She spells each word aloud as she writes the phrase and then takes the children to each word in turn: saying the word, spelling the word, and then asking the children to spell the word with her.

She then points to the first word. 'What is this word?'

'*Ladder*' they chorus.

'And if you saw the word and couldn't remember it, what can you do?'

'Go down the line to the ladder in the picture', they say.

'Right. And what's this word?', pointing to the word *the*.

'*The*', they chorus again. She repeats the process with *bear's* and *sitting* and then asks for the whole phrase, but calls on Hannah.

'*The bear's sitting*', says Hannah.

'Who thinks she's right?' asks Judith. The children's hands go up.

Judith continues to elicit words from the children, continuing the pattern as before, examining each word and regularly reviewing all of them.

By the end of the session, the following list has been accumulated, and the children can say each word as the teacher points to it. Judith finishes by asking them to see if they notice any of the words in the books they are taking home for the evening to share with their parents. As they break, an older child who has been recording the words on a computer saves the file and hands her the disk.

ladder	sitting	bear's	apples
teddy bear	apple tree	basket	grass
tree	tree	basket	apple core
gate	ladder	apple with a leaf	
tree trunk	little trees		
half-eaten apple	bear	apple	
core	leaf	trunk	teddy
apple	little	half-eaten	trees

The following day, as the children enter the classroom, some of them go up to the picture and look at the words, saying them to each other and following words they don't remember down the lines to the objects those words are connected to.

Again, the children sit near the poster. Judith has them read the words, using the picture to help them locate the referents for the words.

Judith has taken the file of words that were shaken out of the picture, put them into a large font, and printed them out, making a set of word cards. She gives each child a complete set. Now she asks the children to read their set and, if they can't remember a word, to go to the poster, find the word and trace it down to the part of the picture it represents.

Much activity ensues. The children peer at the words, saying them, usually aloud, to themselves. Occasionally, they ask Judith if they are right, and she sends them to the picture to find out for themselves. Soon children are getting up and down, holding a word card and locating the word on the chart.

She then asks them for sentences about the picture as a whole, and gets sentences like 'The teddy bear is sitting in the countryside' and 'There are apples all over the place.' One child asks a question. Pointing to an apple core, she wonders 'Who do you suppose ate that apple? Can teddy bears eat apples?' Judith records the sentences, and they read them together before closing the session.

The following morning she again reviews the chart with the children. Then she asks them to take out their word cards and put words together according to how they are spelled. Here are some of the categories they came up with:

Iain: '*Tree* and *trees* and *ladder* have two letters just alike.'

Teacher: 'Super, can you point to the letters?' Iain does so.

Teacher: 'Did anyone else put words together for the same reason? Rebecca?'

Rebecca: 'I put *apple* and *teddy* together because one has two *p*s together and the other has two *d*s together.'

Judith calls on Victoria, who has been patiently waving her hand.

Victoria: '*Apples*, too, *apples* has two just alike.'

Brian adds: 'I put *teddy* and *ladder* together because they have two *d*s in the middle.'

Teacher: 'Let's look at *apple* and *apples*. How are they the same and how are they different?' Several children volunteer, and she calls on Dylan.

Dylan: 'They're spelled the same except for the circles on the end.'

Teacher: 'Which one has the circle, Dylan, *apple* or *apples*?'

Dylan shouts: '*Apples*!'

Zoe: '*S*, *apples* has an *s*. And *apple* is just one apple and *apples* is two apples.'

The sharing continues. Judith pauses when *tree* and *trunk* are placed together because of the *tr* at the beginning. She asks, 'Now, think very carefully.' She takes a pair of scissors and cuts a bit off one edge. 'I just trimmed this piece of paper. How do you think the word *trim* will be spelled at the beginning?'

The children are puzzled for a minute, and then hands begin to go up. Judith waits until nearly all the pupils have an idea, and then calls on Brendan.

Brendan: 'Like *tree*!'

Ricardo: 'Probably with a *tr*, 'cause *trim* sounds like the others at the beginning.'

They discuss Brendan's and Ricardo's answers, and then Judith writes *trim* on a blank poster near the chart.

They all read the set of words on the chart once more and end for the day. Judith finishes by asking the children to see if they notice any words that begin like *tree*, *trunk* and *trim* in the books they are taking home for the evening to share with their parents. If they find any, to remember them and they will add them to the new poster tomorrow.

We have been visiting with Judith and her class during the week of 14 October. (The school has been in session for around six weeks since the summer holiday.) Judith was using a teaching strategy called the picture-word module, a device for eliciting words in the children's listening/speaking vocabulary so that those words can be studied and mastered and, through classification, be a basis for the early exploration of phonics.

SCENARIO 2: THE SOUND LABORATORY

The children in Mr Harrison's Year 4 class enter their room after lunch to find an array of glasses, bottles, bells, wooden boxes of different sizes, some with holes in them, tuning forks, xylophones and small wooden flutes. These objects are spread about the room, and the students spend a few minutes playing with them, creating a most horrendous sound. Mr Harrison watches and listens.

After a few minutes, the students begin to settle down, and one of them asks, 'What's going on here, Mr Harrison? It looks like you've turned the place into an orchestra.'

'Well, in a way', he smiles. 'Actually, for the next few weeks this is going to be our sound laboratory.' He moves across the room and picks up a box and plucks one of the wires that is fastened to it. Simultaneously, he uses a spoon to strike a soft-drink bottle on the desk next to him. 'Do you notice anything about these sounds?' he asks, and repeats his plucking and striking.

'Hey,' says one of the girls, 'they sound the same, but different.'

'Do it again, please' suggests one of the students, and Mr Harrison obliges. Soon all of the students have noticed that the sound is at the same pitch or level.

'Your problem', explains Mr Harrison, 'is to find out what makes sound vary and to describe that variation. Given the limitations of the devices we have in this room, I want you to organize yourselves to conduct some experiments and present me with sets of principles that you think describe the variations. When you're finished, I want you to be able to describe to me how you would design an instrument with certain capabilities. I'll tell you what I want the instrument to be able to do, and you can tell me how to make it. Then we'll begin to test your ideas. Now, I think we ought to organize ourselves into groups and decide how we're going to go about this. Does anybody have any ideas?'

'Well,' Catherine ventures, 'I've noticed that the things are made out of five different kinds of materials. Maybe we could get into five groups and each group would experiment with those for a while. Then we could share what we've learned with the other group and compare their thinking with ours. After that we could decide what to do next.'

Someone joins in with another suggestion, and the class spends the next half hour planning how the study will begin.

SCENARIO 3: THE EARLY INQUIRY INTO WRITTEN LANGUAGE

Five-year-old Brendan sits in a circle with the other children in his school's technology base. In front of each child is an Acorn 3000 computer, networked to the others and to the teacher's workstation, whose displays are projected to large screens on opposite sides of the room. On the monitors are the screens of Pendown Plus, blank and ready to receive words. In the middle of a circle is a model that has been created by the children of the Wollaton School neighbourhood. Houses and shops built of card sit on a map painted on large sheets of newsprint.

The teacher, Jeanie Jones, opens a discussion of the model with the children, speaking with them about the walks they have taken, the things they have observed, and the decisions about what has been selected for inclusion in the model. Then she says 'Now, let's talk about what we've learned and write down some of those things.' Brendan raises his hand, but Ms Jones calls on Suleng.

'I think we found that parts of the community have houses and other parts have shops.'

'Let me type that in for you' says Ms Jones, and she does, using a large font. The children watch as the words appear on their screens. Then Ms Jones places her cursor under the first word and moves it as the children repeat the words. She then asks them to save the sentence on their own floppy disks under the file name 'Our neighbourhood'. The children have saved files before, but it is a few minutes before the task is accomplished with help from each other, Ms Jones, and the support assistant, Mrs Trent.

Then another student has an idea.

'We found that we have three doctors, four dentists and one pet hospital.' Again Ms Jones taps in the sentence, and the students read it together as she moves her cursor under the words. She then has them read both sentences and then save them onto their disks. Now she asks the children to read the sentences to themselves, moving their cursors from word to word as she has done.

The process continues. Two more sentences are added, read and saved, and the children read the four sentences together:

'I think we found that parts of the community have houses and other parts have shops.'

'We found that we have three doctors, four dentists and one vet.'

'Some of us live close enough to the school to walk, but the others have to take the bus.'

'The parks are where the houses are, not where the shops are.'

Ms Jones announces that they will stop at this point. She asks the children to print out their files and cut the words apart. They collect their piles of words into envelopes and take them, with their disks, back to their tables. She says they will take a little break and then come back and sort the words into groups according to how the words begin. By this time Brendan is bursting and she recognizes him. He says '*Doctor* and *dentist* start with the same letter and they sound the same at the beginning.' She smiles and says 'That's right, Brendan, and that's exactly the kind of thing I want you to notice when you sort the words. We're studying our neighbourhood, our computers, and learning to read, all at the same time.'

SCENARIO 4: THE INQUIRY INTO POETRY

Mary Thomas opens the course in her Year 10 English class by presenting the students with 12 poems that she has selected from a set of 100 poems representing the works of prominent contemporary poets. She organizes the students into pairs, asks them to read the poems and then classify them by structure, style and themes. As they classify the poems, they also prepare to report their categories to the other students so that each pair can compare their classifications with those of the other students.

Working together, the class accumulates a list of the ways they have discriminated structure, style and theme. Then Ms Thomas presents the pairs of students with another dozen poems which they examine, fitting them into their existing categories and expanding the categories as necessary. This process is repeated until all students are familiar with nearly 50 poems.

She then gives the students several other tasks: one is to decide how particular themes are handled by style and structure and vice versa (whether style and structure are correlated with each other and with themes). Another task is to build hypotheses about whether some groups of poems were written by particular authors using distinctive combinations of style, structure and theme.

Only then does she pass out the anthologies and books of critical analysis that are used as the textbooks of the course, asking students to test their hypotheses about authorship and also to find out if the scholars of poetry employ the same categories they have been developing as pairs.

Theme

Learning experiences are composed of content, process and social climate. As learners we create for and with our children opportunities to explore and build important areas of knowledge, to develop powerful tools for learning and to live in humanizing social conditions.

As we saw in the preceding scenarios, our toolbox is the models of teaching – actually models for learning – that simultaneously define the nature of the content, the learning strategies and the arrangements for social interaction that create the learning environments of our students.

Through the selection of appropriate models, content can become conceptual rather than particular; process can become constructive inquiry instead of passive reception, and social climate can become expansive not restrictive. Our choices depend on the range of our active teaching repertoire and our efforts to expand it by developing new models and studying those developed by others.

Interestingly, the most powerful models of teaching adapt flexibly to a wide spectrum of curriculum areas and types of learners. They work when teaching phonics and physics. They help both the 'gifted' and those most 'at risk' of failure. They do not tolerate socioeconomic or gender differences as inhibitors of learning but, instead, capitalize on them. Their effects are enhanced by variety in cultural and linguistic background.

Our purpose in this book is to introduce some of the array of models of teaching that have been developed, polished and studied during the modern era of educational research. We hope that teachers, advisers, inspectors, teacher trainers and educational researchers will study these models. If they do, they will discover elegant modes of teaching that have great power for learners. Well implemented, some of these models both accelerate rates of learning, sometimes several times, and also bring within the reach of students types of conceptual control and modes of inquiry that are impossible to generate through many of the most common methods of teaching, such as 'recitation' or 'chalk and talk'.

This book owes its existence to all those great teacher-researchers who created models of teaching that empower children as learners. Bruce Joyce's original formulation of families of teaching strategies (*Models of Teaching*, Joyce and Weil 1972) is now in its fifth edition. During its first quarter century it has influenced the professional development of two generations of American teachers and improved the classroom experience and academic achievement of tens of thousands of students. We have similar aspirations for this book, *Models of Learning – Tools for Teaching*, which we hope will empower more teachers, more students, in more places.

Three ideas guided our selection of content: first, we present a restricted range of models; there are many other well-researched models of teaching. However, the models we have selected represent a powerful initial repertoire for most teachers in most situations. Second, we have also emphasized, in some detail, that models of teaching are in fact models of learning. And third, conscious of the debate in the UK and elsewhere over the 'quality of teaching', we argue strongly that excellence in teaching and learning transcends the dichotomy between whole-class teaching and individual instruction.

We are convinced that 'models of learning and tools for teaching' are culturally independent, being as appropriate to educational situations as diverse as the USA, the UK, India, Israel, Japan, South Africa, Sweden, Australia and Hong Kong. That has been our personal experience. We therefore make no apology for citing examples of high quality teaching from around the world, and using words such as *instruction* and *pedagogy* to emphasize that teaching and learning are independent of location and curriculum content.

Our common interest is school improvement, by which we mean the strenuous and relentless search for more effective ways of educating our young people. We remain convinced that the core of school improvement is the process of teaching and learning. Without this as a central focus, we may well have more satisfied teachers, better run schools, more textbooks, smaller class sizes, but *not* students who know more and learn more easily.

Looking now to the structure of the book, in Chapter 1 we discuss our rationale for establishing the school as a community of learners. This is an argument that we find easy to make – which should come as no surprise to anyone who has read so far. We then provide an extended example of a primary school that we have come to know well and that exemplifies our aspirations. We know of few better schools anywhere than Hempshill Hall school, Nottingham.

In Chapter 2 we provide a succinct overview of the four families of teaching models from which our basic repertoire is drawn. Although brief, we have attempted to provide sufficient information for those who wish to understand the logic of the approach and wish to pursue a more exotic and extensive repertoire.

In Chapters 3 to 10 we describe our basic repertoire of models of learning and their main features. Each chapter follows a similar pattern. We first provide a series of scenarios that illustrate each model of learning and teaching. A section outlining the model in general is followed by a more specific description of its main phases. A short section that reviews relevant research follows, and each chapter concludes with a brief 'reflection'. Each of these final sections includes a diagram that illustrates the instructional and nurturant effects of the model, and a table that outlines its main components or syntax. The concept we refer to as 'syntax' depicts the structure of a model – its major elements or phases and how they are put together. Some models, such as concept attainment, have relatively fixed structures within which some of the elements or phases need to follow each other for maximum effectiveness. Others – such as the inductive model – have a rolling or wavelike structure where phrases are recycled. Where appropriate, in a few chapters some additional sections are included that elaborate particular aspects of the model.

In Chapters 11 and 12 we again broaden the focus beyond the individual teacher and classroom. In Chapter 11 we further elaborate the link between teaching and learning by illustrating how the various models of teaching described in the book can be used to support the development of the six classes of learning identified by Robert Gagné. In Chapter 12 we suggest ways in which teachers working in pairs and as an entire staff can learn new models of teaching. Our purpose is to engage with the realities and challenges of acquiring a repertoire of models and to stress the importance of establishing the workplace conditions necessary to allow teachers sufficient mastery to impact on the learning of their students.

In the Coda we return to our larger theme by attempting to point out as clearly as possible the importance of our argument for policymakers. We continue to despair at the politicization of the educational debate on both sides of the Atlantic. The 'letter to policymakers' is our attempt to redress the balance.

In a series of appendices we first provide an explanation of 'effect size'. This is a statistical technique that revolutionizes the accessibility of the debate on the impact of innovation on student performance, and relegates 'league tables' once and for all to the educational Middle Ages. In discussing the research on models of teaching we refer in a number of chapters to the 'magnitude of effect' that we can expect when using one teaching strategy rather than another. In Appendix 2 we also present a series of peer coaching guides for each of our basic models. These are designed to help teachers think about the moves of the model as they practise them.

As we conclude this initial rehearsal of our theme, it is important to remind ourselves that each model is an inquiry into learning and teaching: this is the basis for much of their strength. Rather than being formulas to be followed slavishly, each model encourages us to study how our students learn and makes us reflective action researchers in our classrooms. In so doing we reshape environments for teaching and select new learning experiences for our students.

We are grateful to the great teacher-researchers who give us this rich professional heritage. In the search for an increasing range of teaching strategies, they both exercised their splendid imaginations and pursued their ideas tenaciously.

1 An inquiry into learning and teaching

Last September, a hundred years ago, I thought teaching was one job with a few variations. I had an image of the one kind of teaching I could do well with the one kind of student I could see myself teaching well. It turned out that it is 20 jobs to do with 20 different personalities.

A beginning teacher to Bruce Joyce, December 1995

Thinking about the roles that make up teaching can make you dizzy. Just for starters, these roles include helping students grow in understanding, knowledge, self-awareness, moral development and the ability to relate to others. Simultaneously we are managers of learning, curriculum designers, facilitators, counsellors, evaluators and, reluctantly, disciplinarians. To the best of our ability, we modulate across roles according to individual and group needs as we select and create learning experiences for all our students.

Creating these learning experiences requires a large repertoire of teaching strategies. So, as teachers, we have another built-in role: acquiring more ways of teaching so that we can select the best possible learning experiences for each curriculum purpose and group of students; and by doing this, we become increasingly skilful in the use of these strategies.

Consider these four teachers at work on the first day of school.

SCENARIO I: YEAR I

In a Year 1 class, the children are gathered around a table on which is a candle and a jar. The teacher, Jackie Wiseman, lights the candle and, after it has burned brightly for a minute or two, places the jar carefully over the candle. It grows dim, flickers and goes out. Then she produces another candle and a larger jar, and the exercise is repeated. The candle goes out, but more slowly. Jackie produces two more candles and jars of different sizes, and the children light the candles, place the jars over them, and the flames slowly go out. 'Now we're going to develop some ideas about what has just happened', she says. 'I want you to ask me questions about those candles and jars and what you just observed.' The children begin. She gently helps them rephrase their questions or plan experiments. When one asks, 'Would the candles burn longer with an even bigger jar?' Jackie responds, 'How might we find out?' Periodically she will ask them to dictate to her what they know and the questions they have. Then she writes what they say on large sheets of paper. Their own words will be the content of their first study of reading.

SCENARIO 2: YEAR 1

Next door the children are seated in pairs. In front of them are a pile of small objects. Each pair of children also has a magnet. Their teacher, Jan Fisher, smiles at them and explains that the 'U-shaped' object is called a magnet. 'We're going to find out something about this thing we call a magnet. We'll begin by finding out what it does when it's held close to different things. So I want you to explore with your magnet. Find out what happens when you bring it close to or touch the things in front of you with it. And sort the other objects according to what happens.' Like Jackie, Jan will take notes on the categories they form and use those to begin their study of written vocabulary.

Commentary: scenarios 1 and 2

Jackie is beginning her year with the model of teaching we call 'Inquiry training'. The model begins by having the students encounter what will be, to them, a puzzling situation. Then by asking questions and conducting experiments, they build ideas and test them. Jackie will study their inquiry and plan the next series of activities to build a community that can work together to explore their world.

Jan has begun with the model we call 'Inductive thinking'. That model begins by presenting the children with information or having them collect information and engage in classifying. As the children develop categories, in this case, concerning the response of objects to what the kids will eventually learn to call a magnetic field, they will build hypotheses to test. Jan will study how they think, what they see and don't see, and help them learn to tackle other topics and questions as a community of inductive thinkers.

SCENARIO 3: TENTH GRADE

Mariam True's tenth grade social studies class begins with a videotape taken in a California courtroom, where litigation is being conducted over whether a mother can prevent a father and their 12-year-old son from having time together. The parents are divorced and have joint custody of their son, who lives with the mother.

The tape presents the opening arguments in the case. Mariam then asks the students to generate, individually, the issues as they see them and request further information about the situation. She then asks them to share the issues and questions they see; she requests each student to accumulate the ideas and questions that all the students share under headings of 'issues' and 'questions'. They find it necessary to develop another category called 'positions and values', because many of the students articulated positions during the sharing exercise.

The inquiry will continue by watching more segments of the tape and analysing several abstracts of similar cases that Mariam has collected for them. One such case is their first homework assignment. Gradually, through the week, Mariam leads the students to develop sets of policy statements and identify the values that underlie the various possible policies. As the study proceeds she will be studying how well the students are able to clarify facts, distinguish value positions from one another, and discuss differences between seemingly opposing values and policy positions. She, too, is beginning the development of a learning inquiry and is herself an inquirer into her students and their learning.

SCENARIO 4: YEAR 9

Now let's move to Gill Murray's English class, which opens with a scene from the film, *Kes*. The students share their reactions to the setting, the actions, and the characters who are introduced in the scene. Among the students a variety of different views are expressed, and when the students want to defend their interpretations or argue against the ideas of others, Gill announces that, for the time being, she wants to preserve their differences so that they can inquire into them. She then passes out copies of the novel of the same name by the author Barry Hines and asks them to begin reading it. During the week she will lead them to develop an inquiry into the social issues presented by the book and film and, simultaneously, by comparing the film with the book, to study the devices used by the author and by the film-makers. She will watch closely to determine what issues and devices they see and don't see as she builds her community of learners.

Commentary: scenarios 3 and 4

Mariam has opened her class with the Jurisprudential model of teaching, which is designed to lead students to the study of public policy issues and their own values.

Gill has begun to introduce her students to the Group Investigation Model, a very powerful cooperative learning model she has used to design her course. The model begins with a confrontation with information that will lead to an area of inquiry, and the students inquire into their perceptual worlds, including similarities and differences in perception as the inquiries proceed.

Keeping these four teachers and classrooms in mind, let's return to the discussion of our work. As we teach, we try to find out what learning has taken place in our classrooms and what readiness there is for new learning. But teachers cannot crawl inside students' heads and look around – we have to infer what is inside from what we can see and hear. Our educated guesses are part of the substance of our profession as we try to construct in *our* minds the pictures of what our students are experiencing. The never-ending cycles of arranging environments, providing tasks and building pictures of the minds of the students makes the character of teaching. This inquiry into mind and environment never completes itself, for the results of these inquiries tell us what next to say and do with our students.

The inquiry process that guides the creation of learning experiences is exactly the same in the secondary phase of education and in the university as it is with young children. The maths teacher and the professor of physics arrange environments, provide tasks and try to learn what is going on in the minds of their students, just as does the teacher who first introduces reading and writing to her students.

The challenge of designing learning experiences is the central substance of the study of teaching. The quest for ways to help people learn more efficiently, and the design of environments that make this learning possible, guide the research that has spawned the range of models we use to design learning experiences. These models are the products of teacher-researchers who have beaten a path for us and given us a head start in our personal and collaborative inquiries.

Currently we operate on several theses about the product of these inquiries. The first thesis is that *there exists a considerable array of alternative approaches to teaching.* Many of these are practical and implementable in classrooms and schools where persons have the combination of will and skill. Further, these models of teaching are sufficiently different from one another that various kinds of outcomes result when they are used (Joyce and Weil 1996). Thus the second thesis is that *methods make a difference in what is learned as well as how it is learned.* Particular methods boost certain outcomes and diminish others, but rarely do they guarantee some while obliterating the rest. The third thesis is that *students are a powerful part of the learning experience being created, and students react differently to any given teaching method.* Combinations of personality, aptitudes, interpersonal skills and previous achievement contribute to configurations of learning styles so that no two people react exactly the same way to any one model of teaching.

A primary task of teachers and school staffs is to equip themselves with a variety of models of teaching that they can bring into play for different purposes, models they can employ and adapt for different learners, combining them artfully to create classrooms and learning communities of variety and depth. To do this requires clarity about what models exist, about what they can accomplish, and about how different students will react to them. To use a variety of models of teaching comfortably and effectively requires study and practice, but by concentrating on one or two at a time we can expand our repertoires quite easily. One key to getting good at them is to use them as tools of inquiry. A second key is that models of teaching are really *models of learning.* As we help students acquire information, ideas, skills, values, ways of thinking and means of expressing themselves, we are also teaching them how to learn. *In fact, the most important long-term outcome of teaching may be the students' increased capabilities to learn more easily and effectively in the future, both because of the knowledge and skill they have acquired and because they have mastered learning processes.*

Thus models of teaching have a cumulative effect on learning because students acquire multiple strategies for learning; students also become part of a community designed to support increasing competency year by year at the individual and group levels. In other words, increasing the range of learning experiences provided in our schools increases the likelihood of more students becoming more adept learners. In addition, every year a student attends a school in which every classroom provides a powerful learning environment increases his or her opportunity to achieve academically.

Let's look now at the nurturant relationship between classrooms and schools as learning communities and at the symbiotic relationship between individual and group learning.

SETTINGS FOR LEARNING: SCHOOLS, CLASSES, GROUPS AND INDIVIDUALS

We learn in human *settings* – assemblages of children and adults created for the purpose of learning. The fact of assembly is more important than the place we usually call school, as is apparent today when people can easily relate to one another electronically. Because we can communicate so effectively through media, we can 'assemble' without being in close physical proximity.

However, the familiar schoolhouse has great importance, for within it and in cooperation with our surrounding community, staff and students generate social climates that influence the energy that is focused on education and the substance and process of that education. Some schools are not only more *effective* than others in drawing the students together to learn (see, for example, Rutter *et al.* 1979; Mortimore *et al.* 1988; Levine and Lezotte 1990), they also pull the students toward specific kinds of inquiry. The social climate of great schools energizes all their students in particular ways: for example the Bronx School of Science, Cranmore, in the USA, or Summerhill in England.

In the USA in the 1930s, the schools that belonged to the Progressive Education Association developed social climates and curricula that helped the entire student body learn to cooperate, to pursue academic inquiry and to develop self-reliance. In Lawrence Kohlberg's (1981) work with *Just Schools*, the exploration of morality came to be a hallmark, and democratic process (with the continuing exploration of social values) became normative.

In England, the work of Henry Morris in the 1940s (through the establishing of community colleges in Cambridgeshire) typified a commitment to a particular style of educational and community ethos.

Similarly, the work of Sir Alec Clegg in the West Riding of Yorkshire during the 1960s and 1970s exemplified how a coherent educational philosophy can influence not only the structure and curriculum of schooling but also the regeneration of communities.

Today we can use various models of teaching to design the social climates and curricula of schools, fostering independence, rigorous inquiry, collaboration, the development of social values and self-esteem. Because social climate can be so powerful, its design has considerable importance and should not be left to chance.

The *class* as an educational group – meaning a particular classroom with a single teacher – is the most familiar setting in most schools, although there are many designs for schools where the single-teacher classroom is not dominant. As a practical matter, however, the class is where most formal education takes place in today's societies, whether students spend all or most of their time in one class or are reassembled in classes throughout the day. Whatever curricular frameworks are followed, the actual curriculum is what teachers generate in classes. Oddly, the public thinks of the school as the setting for education: they send their children to *school* not to a particular class. Educators, however, more often think of the class.

Because of the centrality of the class as the centre of education in most schools, the question of how to teach the class dominates discussions of method. Today many of those discussions centre around whether 'whole class' or 'group activity' should dominate, or what should be the balance between whole class, small group and individual activities. Settling that question leads us to the broader question of what will work best for children, because it is the models of learning and teaching that are chosen, rather than the grouping arrangements adopted, that will directly affect student achievement. Thus the operational repertoire of the teachers is the critical element in the calculus of effects. For one can teach whole classes well or badly, organize collaborative groups well or badly, and provide direct individual instruction well or badly.

The traditional 'chalk and talk, drill and recite' method (CTDR) still dominates the repertoire of most teachers and the minds of many critics of education. Unfortunately CTDR falls terribly short of reaching the aspirations of today's schools. In the United States, where two of us live, a combination of recitation and lecture leaves about one-third of the students unable to complete secondary education, and another one-fifth unable to read and write to a standard that permits them to hold jobs requiring literacy. It is a very poor format from which to promote outstanding achievement or to tend individual student differences. Recent government reports on student achievement in reading and maths in England and Wales suggest that the situation may be similar in these countries too. Furthermore, the central issue for school staff, governors and policymakers to face is that the poor track record of CTDR in student achievement holds true whether the educational group is 'small group' or 'whole class'.

The more efficient models of teaching *assume* that the whole class will be organized to pursue common learning objectives within which individual differences in achievement are comfortably accommodated. Thus their creators have a vision of the whole class and a vision of small group work and individual work as part of the overall educational scheme. In these classes, students are taught directly models for learning that they use when working as members of the class community, when working in small collaborative groups and when working as individuals.

In the best scenario, the whole school is a centre of learning for teachers, parents and students. Let's visit such a school where an overarching collaborative inquiry model has been used to design the educational environment.

HEMPSHILL HALL SCHOOL

The following section was generated jointly by four people: Bruce Joyce and Emily Calhoun, who visited the school several times during October 1996 and made videotapes of lessons they taught while there; David Hopkins, who has an ongoing relationship with the school; and Marcia Puckey, the head teacher. Documents from the school files were drawn upon extensively, as was the report from the Office for Standards in Education (OFSTED) on their inspection of the school in 1994. The OFSTED report was the product of the government inspection team responsible for assessing the quality of the school. The six-member team spent a week in the school; examined its documents pertaining to curriculum, instruction, management and assessments; observed 121 lessons or parts of lessons; watched assemblies; held discussions with teachers; interviewed the governors (school lay council); attended a meeting of 65 parents; examined the responses by 114 parents to a questionnaire; held planned discussions with students from Year 6; and listened to a range of pupils read.

The other day – an otherwise ordinary October day in 1996 – we visited Hempshill Hall primary school in Bulwell, Nottingham. We have visited on several occasions since, videotaping lessons we taught for our storehouse of tapes depicting the inductive model of teaching in action.

The school serves about 350 children from the working-class community of Bulwell. About 60 per cent of the children live in the catchment (immediate neighbourhood), a pleasant area of tidy homes. Within the catchment, most families are two-parent households. The majority of the fathers have marketable skills and their employment provides a comfortable living. Most of the mothers left school early, married young and have few skills that are marketable in today's workplaces, although they will be quite young when their children reach the age where intensive parenting consumes less and less time.

About 40 per cent of the students who attend Hempshill Hall come from outside the neighbourhood. The economic and family situation of these children who live outside the catchment area is quite different. The majority of these children come from households where the mother raises the children alone, and many are in public housing. Few of their mothers have marketable skills.

About 30 per cent of the children in the school, most of them from the homes outside the catchment, receive free (government-subsidized) lunches.

The school has a head and ten full-time teaching staff. There are four paid teaching assistants. In addition there are five assistants-in-training under a programme developed by the head, who capitalized on the need by many of the mothers to begin to develop marketable skills.

In addition, the head has made arrangements with several teacher education programmes to provide experience for student teachers. There are usually a half-dozen student teachers working in some capacity in the school.

Perhaps most important, 60 parent volunteers work in the school each week for about a half-day to two days each. Again, the head has capitalized on the nature of the community, drawing into the school those parents who have the willingness and time to be a major part of the school community. As the head put it: 'You must be totally inclusive. Lots of people can help out if you will only provide the avenues and make them welcome.'

The school as a social system: collaboration, inquiry, responsibility

Hempshill Hall is packed with activity, much too much to report in less than a full-length book devoted only to the school. But what we observed is relevant to the framework we have been presenting about school- and class-level settings and group and individual-level dimensions of education.

Mrs H. Marcia Puckey, the head teacher, has worked with the staff and parents to develop a thoroughgoing process for building a collaborative, energetic social system. One in which school staff, parents and students share responsibility for excellence in academic, social and personal development of the children. From the letter to parents: 'We are all equal partners at Hempshill Hall. We welcome parents who want to be fully involved in school life.'

The social system has many dimensions. These are a few of them:

Orientation of the parents and children to the school. Meetings between parents, children and school begin before the children have reached school age. In the autumn of each year there are a series of meetings designed to build the student-parent-school partnership.

The Thursday club. Parents in the community of children not yet in school are invited to bring their children to the school on Thursdays so that both parents and children can become accustomed to the school.

Importantly, the Thursday club inaugurates for families the orientation process; it provides them with opportunities to 'talk' to the school.

The staff has organized its actions to ensure that parents are welcomed into the school. Parents evidently do feel like an integral part of the school community because approximately one person from every six families is successfully recruited to work as assistants to the teachers.

School assemblies. Two or three times a week the entire school gathers as an assembly, led by Stuart Harrison who is the deputy head, and a play is presented by a group of students. Many of the plays involve a considerable amount of improvisation and have slowly developing story lines. The assembly brings together the students as a whole-school community, provides an opportunity to develop them into a civil, polite audience, and, incidentally, means that each year they are participants in or audience to about 70 plays. The OFSTED report comments:

> Spiritual development is encouraged in the broadest sense and permeates the life of the school in a pervasive yet unobtrusive manner. Opportunities are taken to bring out spiritual issues during lessons, as they occur. Regular, well-prepared school and class assemblies take place, often using stories that illustrate values or have a moral content. The assemblies contribute effectively to the school's overall ethos and values.

The process is reminiscent of the model described in Chapter 8 where role playing is used to make values available for study.

Communication and the home–school connection

The reading wallet. Every child in the school is provided with a red vinyl briefcase, called a 'reading wallet', that they carry between home and school. The wallet contains real books and children's work. Parents are encouraged to provide time for their child to read the books at home and are helped in learning how to support their child's reading.

The comment book. An important communication document in each reading wallet is a 'comment book', a notebook in which teachers and parents write back and forth to each other on a weekly basis. If either makes a comment, the other responds. The comments discuss aspects of the children's academic and social progress and ways of helping them move forward.

To get the flavour of the interaction, let's look at the comments between the parents and teacher of a 5-year-old:

4 September [first day of school]
Teacher: '. . . Jessica has chosen some books to share with you, *The Greatest Show on Earth*, *Brown Bear* and *Not Now, Bernard*. She could just concentrate on one or read them all equally. She can keep these as long as she wants – I will probably next share them with her next

Monday.' [This last comment is a reference to the twice-weekly conference with individual students about books they are reading.]

4 September
Father: 'I read *The Greatest Show* with Jessica and her brothers, Jeroen and Dylan. We discussed the story and tried to find out what was happening from the pictures. Jessica enjoyed the story and understood all the pictures.'

5 September
Mother: 'Jessica read Dylan and me the *Brown Bear* book without much help. She also read Jeroen's book *The Red Fox*.'

6 September
Teacher: 'Thank you. Jessica now has her poetry folder and a poem to share with you.'

9 September
Mother: 'Jessica and her younger brother, Dylan, read the poem and she showed us how to shout "all join in". They both enjoyed it, so we read it a few times. She also read us the *Brown Bear* again.'
    Teacher: 'I am pleased Jessica and Dylan enjoyed the poem. Also, it is interesting to learn what other books she is sharing with you. Jessica read *Brown Bear* with me together and she had remembered it really well. On the few occasions she had forgotten what came next, I just needed to jog her memory by beginning the next word and she remembered and carried on. She is bringing home two new books to share.'

14 September
Father: 'Jessica, her brothers and I read *Bill and Pete* . . . Jessica and I read the story and Dylan told us what was happening in the pictures.'
    Mother: 'Jessica, Dylan and Jeroen read *Would You Rather* and enjoyed it.'

17 September
Teacher: 'Jessica shared *Would You Rather* with me today and she remembered quite a lot of it, using the pictures efficiently to help.'

18 September
Mother: 'Jessica played a matching game with Jeroen with words such as *the, they*; *is, in*; *come, comes*. After that, she read his book, *The Book Shop*.'

It is easy to see that the interchange is relatively dense as parents and teachers try to talk to one another over the common objective – helping the child become a successful reader. The teachers feel that the interchanges help extend the influence of the school into reading/writing activities in the home. The parents feel that the process keeps them in close touch with the student–teacher–parent triad that makes education work.

To make the nature of this connection more vivid, here are some excerpts from an interview with the mother:

> The comments make a real difference. They are one of the best things about having my daughter in Hempshill Hall. It really keeps you in touch and also keeps pressure on you as a parent. You feel that you have to read with the children every day because the teacher comments so regularly. It also is interesting to see how Jessica is learning to read. Yesterday, when I asked her about reading her newest book, she said that she could read it 'because all the words were in my head'. What we do now with Jessica adds about three hours a week to her concentration on learning to read.

The curriculum framework. The curriculum is academically rich and integrative. Everything is taught as the achievement of literacy. Reading is taught through real books. School subjects are divided into units that are tackled as experiential and reading/writing inquiries. The curriculum is naturally rather than artificially integrated, i.e. it is organized around related concepts, not around topics. The curriculum, as stated in the letter to parents, is 'based on the programmes of study in the National Curriculum Core Subjects of Mathematics, Science, English and Technology'.

Teaching, learning and working together. A general inquiry model dominates teaching and learning. All teachers and all children follow a scheme where material to be mastered and problems to be solved are presented; children, organized into groups, get to grips with the material and problems. Thus collaborative inquiry is the hallmark of the process, but individual children have responsibility for many strands of learning, and individual differences in achievement are closely monitored. The school as a whole is the educative unit. In this the school is very different from the typical setting where schools assign children to classes in which teachers, working as individuals in miniature schools, progress through the curriculum. At Hempshill Hall everybody is responsible for all the children working toward common goals and using common strategies.

Every effort is made to help the children feel that they are capable and that each is responsible for the learning of all. From the letter to parents: 'We provide a warm, caring, "family style" environment where your child can feel valued, living in harmony with friends – a real extended family unit.' Within the context of the curriculum units, the children and teachers work together to plan specific activities. In a real sense, learning to cooperate, learning to live democratically and learning to collaborate as inquirers – as scholars – fit together in a comfortable whole.

The mode of collaborative inquiry pervasive at Hempshill Hall also greatly diminishes the disciplinary problems typical of the 'chalk and talk, drill and recite' school. 'Discipline' is a matter of bringing the children into the social norms of cooperation, inquiry and mutual respect.

Thus the mode is socialization, rather than the enforcement of a code only tangentially relevant to the teaching/learning process.

The operation of the school is relevant to contemporary discussions about 'whole class' and 'cooperative group' activity. In a very real sense, the entirety of Hempshill Hall Primary is a 'class' whose members co-operate as a whole and within which cooperative groups work within a common framework to pursue excellence. Personal, social and academic growth are perceived to be part of a whole. From the letter to parents: 'Hempshill Hall School has a mission – that all our children shall be happy, live in harmony and achieve success.'

Classes are not isolated educational settings. The classes operate as units where several teachers work together to plan and carry out their project plans and day-to-day inquiries. The familiar image of 'chalk and talk, drill and recite' is absent. Goals are made clear and the whole class works towards common substantive objectives. On a day-to-day basis, the children work from three-quarters to nine-tenths of the time in collaborative groups and as individuals to master those goals and develop their capacity as learners.

Reading and writing are taught from experience records and real books throughout the curriculum. This practice contrasts sharply with that of most schools, where the language arts are taught as a subject, with the product applied in the other curriculum areas. Reading and writing are pervasive activities at Hempshill Hall.

Similarly, technology is a tool to support learning, not an activity in itself. The computer is integrated in the learning of all subjects. Parents are urged to purchase laptop computers for their children and they are extensively used, as are about 40 computers in the school.

Staff planning. The staff work in teams to develop schemes of work that reflect the National Curriculum. However, each scheme is developed as a research activity for the children, and first-hand experiences such as field trips and secondary experiences such as videotapes and films are combined with extensive reading. Products of research are expressed in writing, multimedia presentations and enactments.

Individual learning and responsibility. Individual responsibility and excellence is expected and supported. Individual students do the learning in all schools. In this case, individual projects are included in the curricular units as offshoots of the collaborative inquiry. Unlike some collaborative schools, Hempshill Hall does not make the mistake of generating 'group products' that are not an amalgam of individual inquiries. In addition, individual children develop their own inquiries, doing personal research and developing and testing their own hypotheses.

The tending of individual needs at all levels is a fluid part of the conduct of teaching. Every week, each child has two personal, one-on-one conferences with an adult over his or her individual reading and receives help in setting personal goals and in resolving problems. In the spring of the year, children in Year 2 who have not progressed above Level 1 in reading are identified and receive intensive assistance. In the spring of 1996, ten children out of 52 were so identified. By the end of the school year, only four had not reached Level 2, the stage where children can read simple books independently.

At Hempshill Hall, parents are very much a part of the educational process on a daily basis. The regular exchange of written communication between parents and teachers, and the daily carrying home of books to be read and pieces being written, reinforces everyone's responsibility for educating the child. And on an average day, about ten parent volunteers will be in the school working alongside the teachers.

The OFSTED inspection report. What do the authorities think of Hempshill Hall? Whenever a school deviates from the 'chalk and talk, drill and recite' mode, people in both the UK and the United States ask, sceptically, whether the 'basics' are being neglected. Largely this scepticism is a product of the culturally normative image of teaching which persists despite its terrifying inefficiency. Of course, most people have had more experience with the CTDR model of teaching – the provision of information, oral or written, followed by queries to which one makes oral or written responses – than any other model, and it 'worked' for them.

The inefficiency of the recitation model of teaching is often attributed to the belief that many teachers have drifted away from its use toward the use of permissive, flaccid modes of teaching, modes commonly thought to be promoted by educational reformers working at a distance from the school. There are continuous calls to reassert recitation and drill as the major method of primary education and to eliminate the 'distractions' of inquiry and group work. These beliefs are held by many members of the public, despite the long recorded and current dominance of the recitation model in English-language countries.

Consequently the opinion of external examiners and the evidence of examination or test results become very important whenever a school strives for excellence through collaborative inquiry models. This is the case, even when a school asserts, as Hempshill Hall does in its letter to parents, that 'Although our [academic] aims are traditional, our methods are not always so, and you may find that your children will be taught very differently to the way you were taught at their age. We respect individual differences, and do not normally "drill" whole classes together, regardless of ability.'

With this cultural context in mind, here are some of the products of the external examination of Hempshill Hall primary school, from the OFSTED inspection report in December 1994:

> Standards in reading, writing and speaking and listening, and in number and information technology, are good and sometimes outstanding . . . Pupils use text effectively for learning. They read widely and value reading as a source of information. They read accurately, expressively, and with understanding. Pupils enjoy books and speak warmly of the pleasures of reading . . . Pupils write with the coherence, fluency, and accuracy which is appropriate for their age and

ability and often beyond. As they move through the school, they tackle successfully an increasing range of written work and plan, develop, and re-write their own text where appropriate. They are able to narrate, explain, describe, hypothesise, analyse, assert, compare, question, and deduce. They listen well to others and respond appropriately and sensitively . . .

Pupils handle number well across the curriculum, mentally and in writing. They use measurement effectively in a range of different contexts, particularly in science, technology, and history. They have well-developed calculator skills and interpret statistical data effectively in their work in humanities.

Standards in information technology are good and sometimes outstanding. Pupils create, modify, and present information in English, art, history, and mathematics. They use databases to enhance the quality of their work in history. By Year 6, pupils build and study computer models confidently and control movement and other physical effects in technology.

At the Key Stage 2 assessment, conducted when 10- to 11-year-olds are leaving Year 6, the percentage of pupils achieving Levels 4 and 5 in English was 70, compared with a national average of 48. In maths, the percentage reaching Levels 4 and 5 was 82, compared with a national average of 44.

IN SUMMARY

Whether at the class or school level, the broader the range of teaching approaches and learning experiences arranged for our children, the more likely we are to reach our goal of educating all students. The more strongly learning permeates the setting we call schools – using multiple models across the years of schooling – the more successful we will be.

In the next chapter we introduce the four families of models of teaching, discuss their origins and their underlying theories, and examine the research that has tested them. As you read Chapter 2, think about how the use of models from different families help us better fulfil our multiple responsibilities of creating learning experiences for all students.

2 Families of models of teaching

At first, when people create or find a new model of teaching that works for some purpose, they're so thrilled they try to use it for everything. Our job is to provide some order – finding out what each model can do and building categories to help folks find the tools they need.

Bruce Joyce, again and again in staff meetings from 1965 to the present

Between us, we have been searching continuously for promising approaches to teaching since the late 1950s. The hunt has many facets. We visit schools (about 50 in the last year alone) and classrooms (about 300 last year), interview teachers, study research on teaching and learning, and look at people in teaching roles outside of schools, such as therapists and trainers in industrial, military and athletic or outdoor settings.

We have found models of teaching in abundance. There are simple procedures that students can easily respond to; there are complex strategies that students acquire gradually through patient and skilful instruction. Some aim at specific objectives, while others are broadly useful. Some are quite formal, while others are casual and emergent. Among them, they address a great variety of objectives in the personal, social and academic domains – our major responsibilities as teachers.

In the United States, from the late 1950s until the mid-1970s, research sponsored by foundations, the Federal government and school districts refined long-standing models of teaching and developed new ones to a degree not seen before or since. Some of the research was concentrated on specific curriculum areas, especially English, humanities, science and mathematics.

There was a similar commitment to curriculum development in England during this period. The work of the Schools Council, and the Nuffield Foundation in particular, was highly influential in not only introducing a range of new curricula into the English educational system, but also in establishing a distinctive style of curriculum research and development that focused on the teacher (Stenhouse 1975, 1980; Rudduck and Hopkins 1985). Many of these curriculum projects highlighted the importance of integrating teaching strategies and the learning needs of students into the design of curriculum materials (Hopkins 1987).

During the same period, research on effective teachers and schools shed light on their practices. During the last 20 years, research on mnemonics and cooperative learning has redeveloped and refined models in those areas, and research on training has clarified how people acquire skills and apply (transfer) them to solve problems. Recent work on how students construct knowledge is enriching those models, as is research on how students develop the 'metacognitions' that enable them consciously to improve their strategies for learning.

These models of teaching can be used by individual teachers and by staff as instructional strategies; as guides when planning lessons, units, courses and curricula or when designing classroom activities and instructional materials.

To bring order into the study of the growing storehouse of models, we have grouped them into four families based on the types of learning they promote and on their orientation toward people and how they learn: the information processing family, the social family, the personal family, and the behavioural systems family.

Criteria of practicability were used to select the models from each family that would have considerable utility in instructional settings. Thus the models we draw on have long histories of practice behind them: they have been refined through experience so that they can be used comfortably and efficiently in classrooms and other educational settings. Furthermore, they are adaptable: they can be adjusted to the learning styles of students and to the requirements of subject matter. They have lifetime utility: most are useful across the primary and secondary levels, as well as in university, and are learning tools for life. And finally, there is evidence that they work in enhancing students' ability to learn: all of them are backed by some amount of formal research that tests their theories and their abilities to effect learning. The amount of related research varies from model to model. Some are backed by a few studies while others have a history of literally hundreds of items of research.

THE INFORMATION PROCESSING FAMILY OF MODELS

Information processing models emphasize ways of enhancing the human being's innate drive to make sense of the world by acquiring and organizing data, sensing problems and generating solutions to them, and developing concepts and language for conveying them. Some models in this family provide the learner with information and concepts; some emphasize concept formation and hypothesis testing by the learner; and still others generate creative thinking. A few are designed to enhance general intellectual ability. Many information processing models are useful for studying the self and society, and thus for achieving the personal and social goals of education.

Figure 2.1 displays the developers and redevelopers of seven information processing models. The references section of the book includes the primary works of the developers.

Model	Developer (redeveloper)	Purpose
Inductive thinking (classification)	Hilda Taba (Bruce Joyce)	Development of classification skills, hypothesis building and testing, and understanding of how to build conceptual understanding of content areas.
Concept attainment	Jerome Bruner Fred Lighthall (Bruce Joyce)	Learning concepts and studying strategies for attaining and applying them. Building and testing hypotheses.
Scientific inquiry	Joseph Schwab and many others	Learning the research system of the academic disciplines – how knowledge is produced and organized.
Inquiry training	Richard Suchman (Howard Jones)	Causal reasoning and understanding of how to collect information, build concepts, and build and test hypotheses.
Cognitive growth	Jean Piaget Irving Sigel Constance Kamii Edmund Sullivan	Increase general intellectual development and adjust instruction to facilitate intellectual growth.
Advance organizers	David Ausubel (and many others)	Designed to increase ability to absorb information and organize it, especially in learning from lectures and readings.
Mnemonics	Michael Pressley Joel Levin (and associated scholars)	Increase ability to acquire information, concepts, conceptual systems and metacognitive control of information processing capability.

Figure 2.1 Information processing models

The information processing models help students learn how to construct knowledge. They focus directly on intellectual capability. As the term implies, these models help students operate on information obtained either from direct experience or from mediated sources so that they develop conceptual control over the areas they study. The emphases of the various information processing models are somewhat different, however, in the sense that each one has been designed to enhance particular kinds of thinking.

In Chapters 3 to 6 we share four models from the information processing family: in Chapter 3 the *inductive thinking model* induces students to learn to collect and classify information and to build and test hypotheses. Classification, which is one phase of this model, is probably the basic higher order 'thinking skill' and is certainly a necessary skill for mastering large amounts of information.

In Chapter 4 the *concept attainment model* both helps students learn concepts and also to study how they think. Simultaneously, it leads students to develop concepts and to obtain conceptual control (metacognitive understanding) over their thinking strategies.

In Chapter 5 *synectics* teaches metaphoric thinking – ways of consciously 'breaking set' and generating new ideas.

In Chapter 6 the recently developed *mnemonics models* have raised the process of memorizing to a surprisingly high conceptual level by providing tools students can use to learn and analyse information and gain conscious control of their learning processes and how those processes can be improved.

For maximum effect these models are used in combinations as students learn to inquire into any given topic. The *inductive* model can help students collect and analyse information, while *concept attainment* helps them develop new perspectives on the data. *Synectics* helps students stretch their ideas and reformulate them. And *mnemonics* can help students anchor information and ideas in their long-term memory.

The academic curriculum of our schools requires the acquisition and use of massive amounts of information. The information processing family of models provides students with learning strategies to use in gathering, organizing, summarizing and applying this information, forming and testing hypotheses, making generalizations, and developing concepts that define the content of the disciplines, i.e. how language, mathematics, science and social science work.

THE SOCIAL FAMILY OF MODELS:
BUILDING THE LEARNING COMMUNITY

When we work together, we generate collective energy that we call 'synergy'. The social models of teaching are constructed to take advantage of this phenomenon by building learning communities. Essentially, 'classroom management' is a matter of developing cooperative relationships in the classroom. The development of positive school cultures is a process of developing integrative and productive ways of interacting and norms that support vigorous learning activity.

Figure 2.2 identifies several social models, the persons who have developed and redeveloped them, and their basic purposes.

The social family of models help students learn how to sharpen their own cognitions through interactions with others, how to work productively with individuals who represent a range of personalities, and how to work as a member of a group. In terms of cognitive and academic growth, the models help students use the perspectives of other persons, both individual and group perspectives, to clarify and expand their own thinking and conceptualization of ideas.

As with the information processing family, the emphases of the various models in the social family are somewhat different, in the sense that each one has been designed to enhance particular kinds of thinking and modes of interaction. Among the developed spectrum of models in

Model	Developer (redeveloper)	Purpose
Group investigation	John Dewey Herbert Thelen Shlomo Sharan Rachel Hertz-Lazarowitz	Development of skills for participation in democratic process. Simultaneously emphasizes social development, academic skills and personal understanding.
Social inquiry	Byron Massialas Benjamin Cox	Social problem solving through collective academic study and logical reasoning.
Jurisprudential inquiry	James Shaver Donald Oliver	Analysis of policy issues through a jurisprudential framework. Collection of data, analysis of value questions and positions, study of personal beliefs.
Laboratory method	National Training Laboratory (many contributors)	Understanding of group dynamics, leadership, understanding of personal styles.
Role playing	Fannie Shaftel	Study of values and their role in social interaction. Personal understanding of values and behaviour.
Positive interdependence	David Johnson Roger Johnson Elizabeth Cohen	Development of interdependent strategies of social interaction. Understanding of self–other relationships and emotions.
Structured social inquiry	Robert Slavin and colleagues	Academic inquiry and social and personal development. Cooperative strategies for approaching academic study.

Figure 2.2 Social models

the social family we will look briefly at two models: group investigation (a complex form of cooperative learning) and role playing.

Chapter 7 looks at *group investigation* as a direct route to the development of the community of learners. All the simpler forms of cooperative learning are preparation for the rigorous, active and integrative collective action required in group investigation. John Dewey (1916) developed the idea – extended and refined by a great many teachers and theorists and shaped into powerful definition by Herbert Thelen (1960) – that education in a democratic society should teach democratic process directly. A substantial part of the students' education should be by cooperative inquiry into important social and academic problems. Essentially, the group investigation model provides a social organization within which many other models can be used.

Group investigation has been used in all subject areas, with children of all ages, and even as the core social model for entire schools. The model is designed to lead students to define problems, to explore various perspectives on the problems, and to study together to master information, ideas and skills – while simultaneously developing their social competence. The teacher's primary role in this model is to help organize the group process and discipline it, to help the students find and organize information, and to ensure that there is a vigorous level of activity and discourse.

Chapter 8 examines how *role playing* leads students to understand social behaviour, their roles in social interactions, and ways of solving problems more effectively. Designed by Fannie and George Shaftel (1982) specifically to help students study their social values and reflect on them, role playing also helps students collect and organize information about social issues, develop empathy with others and attempt to improve their social skills. The model asks students to 'act out' conflicts, to learn to take the roles of others and to observe social behaviour. With appropriate adaptation, role playing can be used with students of all ages.

As the term *social* implies, these models help students learn to identify multiple facets of a situation or problem, to understand the reasoning underpinning positions different from their own, and to form disciplined cases and reasoned arguments to support their positions. The interactive mode required by these models also means that students simultaneously practise the complex processes of accessing needed information, gathering information and using their social skills. These models require intense use of listening comprehension skills, of on-your-feet organization of information, of the ability to formulate and ask questions in such a fashion that the information sought will be forthcoming, and of being able to put it all together to resolve tough issues or negotiate new solutions. *Thus students are also practising many of the skills that they will need to participate fully as family members, as citizens and as successful workers.* To equip our students with these models of learning is a great lifetime gift.

THE PERSONAL FAMILY OF MODELS

From birth, we are acted on by the world. Our social environment gives us our language, teaches us how to behave and provides love to us. But our individual selves configure themselves relentlessly and create their own interior environments. Within these interior worlds, each of us creates our identity, and our personalities have remarkable continuity from early in life.

Yet while much within our interior world remains stable, we also have great capacity to change. We are incomplete without others; we can love and receive love, generating perhaps the greatest growth of all. Paradoxically, we also have the capacity to hold tight to behaviour that doesn't work – as if to force the world to yield and make our worst features productive. We can adapt to a wide range of environments. We are the greatest! And we can be mulish!

The personal models of learning begin from the perspective of the selfhood of the individual. They attempt to shape education so that we

Model	Developer	Purpose
Nondirective teaching	Carl Rogers	Building capacity for personal development, self-understanding, autonomy and esteem of self.
Awareness training	Fritz Perls	Increasing self-understanding, self-esteem and capacity for exploration. Development of interpersonal sensitivity and empathy.
Classroom meeting	William Glasser	Development of self-understanding and responsibility to self and others.
Self-actualization	Abraham Maslow	Development of personal understanding and capacity for development.
Conceptual systems	David Hunt	Increasing personal complexity and flexibility in processing information and interacting with others.

Figure 2.3 Personal models

come to understand ourselves better, take responsibility for our education, and learn to reach beyond our current development to become stronger, more sensitive and more creative in our search for high quality lives.

The cluster of personal models pays great attention to the individual perspective and seeks to encourage productive independence, so that people become increasingly self-aware and responsible for their own destinies. Figure 2.3 displays the models and their developers.

In the personal models of teaching, the emphasis is on the unique character of each human being and the struggle to develop as an integrated, confident and competent personality. The goal is to help each person 'own' his/her development and to achieve a sense of self-worth and personal harmony. The models that comprise this family seek to develop and integrate the emotional and intellectual aspects of personality. In Chapter 9, 'Learning through counselling', we share some examples of how one teacher has used Rogers' nondirective model with a whole class of students and with an individual student.

THE BEHAVIOURAL SYSTEMS FAMILY OF MODELS

A common theoretical base – most commonly called social learning theory, but also known as behaviour modification, behaviour therapy and cybernetics – guides the design of the models in this family. The stance taken is that human beings are self-correcting communication systems that modify behaviour in response to information about how successfully tasks are navigated. For example, imagine a human being who is climbing (the task) an unfamiliar staircase in the dark. The first few steps are tentative as the foot reaches for the treads. If the stride is too high, feedback is received as the foot encounters air and has to

Model	Developer	Purpose
Social learning	Albert Bandura Carl Thoresen Wes Becker	The management of behaviour. Learning new patterns of behaviour, reducing phobic and other dysfunctional patterns, learning self-control.
Mastery learning	Benjamin Bloom James Block	Mastery of academic skills and content of all types.
Programmed learning	B. F. Skinner	Mastery of skills, concepts, factual information.
Simulation	Many developers. Carl Smith and Mary Foltz Smith provide guidance through 1960s when design had matured.	Mastery of complex skills and concepts in a wide range of areas of study.
Direct teaching	Thomas Good Jere Brophy Wes Becker Siegfried Englemann Carl Bereiter	Mastery of academic content and skills in a wide range of areas of study.
Anxiety reduction	David Rinn Joseph Wolpe John Masters	Control over aversive reactions. Applications in treatment and self-treatment of avoidance and dysfunctional patterns of response.

Figure 2.4 Behavioural and cybernetic models

descend to make contact with the surface. If a step is too low, feedback results as the foot hits the riser. Gradually behaviour is adjusted in accordance with the feedback until progress up the stairs is relatively comfortable.

Capitalizing on knowledge about how people respond to tasks and feedback, psychologists (see especially Skinner 1953) have learned how to organize task and feedback structures to make it easy for human beings' self-correcting capability to function. The result includes programmes for reducing phobias, for learning to read and compute, for developing social and athletic skills, for replacing anxiety with relaxation, and for learning the complexities of intellectual, social and physical skills necessary to pilot an aeroplane or a space shuttle. Because these models concentrate on observable behaviour and clearly defined tasks, and on methods for communicating progress to the student, this family of teaching models has a very large foundation of research. Figure 2.4 displays six models and their developers.

The behavioural systems family, based on the work of B. F. Skinner and the cybernetic training psychologists (Smith and Smith 1966), has the largest literature of the four families. Studies range from programmed instruction to simulations and include training models (Joyce and Showers 1983) and methods derived directly from therapy (Wolpe and Lazarus 1966).

There is a great deal of research on the application of social learning theory to instruction (Becker and Gersten 1982), training (Smith and Smith 1966) and simulations (Boocock and Schild 1968). The behavioural technologists have demonstrated that they can design programmes for both specific and general goals (Becker and Gersten 1982) and also that the effective application of those techniques requires extensive cognitive activity and precise interactive skills (Spaulding 1970).

You may find the results of the research on some of these techniques surprising. For example, an analysis by White (1986) examined the results of studies on the application of the DISTAR version of social learning theory to special education. The average effect sizes for mathematics and reading ranged from about one-half to one standard deviation (for a discussion on effect size, see Appendix 1). The effects for moderately and severely handicapped students were similar. Perhaps most important, there were a few studies in which the effects on aptitude (measures of intellectual ability) were included; and where the DISTAR programme was implemented for several years, the effect sizes were 1.0 or above, representing an increase of about 10 points in the standard IQ ratio.

Overall, behavioural techniques are amenable to learners of all ages and to an impressive range of educational goals. In Chapter 10, 'Learning through simulations', we look more closely at one member of this family. We explore the principles of simulation, share examples of various kinds of simulations and relate the framework of the behaviourists to daily classroom management.

DEVELOPING A BROAD TEACHING REPERTOIRE: A FIRM YET DELICATE HAND

As we study the four families of models of teaching, we try to build a mental picture of what each model is designed to accomplish. As we consider when and how to use various combinations of models and, therefore, which learning strategies will get priority for particular units and lessons and groups of students, we take into account the types and pace of learning that are likely to be promoted. We also need to emphasize that each model has both instructional and nurturant effects. For example, while a model such as inductive teaching will directly enhance a student's range of concept building strategies, it will also at the same time increase their tolerance of ambiguity and awareness of alternative ways of turning information into knowledge. We saw this vividly during our visits to Hempshill Hall school.

We draw on the research to help us determine the sizes and kinds of effects each model has had in its history so that we can estimate its productivity if we use it properly. Sometimes decision making is relatively easy because one model just stands out as though it is crafted for a given purpose. For example, synectics is immediately useful in helping students learn to write metaphorically – for example, in using a metaphor to organize a written composition.

The decision is more complicated when there are several models of teaching that can achieve the same objective. For example, information can be acquired through inductive inquiry or from readings and lectures developed around advance organizers. (Advance organizers, as a model of teaching, assist in the preparation of a lecture or presentation; as a model of learning, they enable the student to make meaning out of such a presentation.) Or the two models can be blended.

The more models of teaching you control, the broader the repertoire available for you to design programmes of learning for your students. Consider a programme to teach students a new language. One of the early tasks when learning a new language is to develop an initial vocabulary. The link-word method has been dramatically successful in initial vocabulary acquisition, in some cases helping students acquire and retain words as much as twice as fast as normal (Pressley *et al.* 1982), making it a good choice for use early in the programme. Students need to acquire skills in reading, writing and conversation which are enhanced by an expanded vocabulary, then other models that generate practice and synthesis can be used.

To make matters even more complicated, we need to acknowledge, thankfully, that students are not identical. What helps one person learn a given thing more efficiently may not help another as much. Fortunately there are very few known cases where an educational treatment that helps a given type of student a great deal has serious damaging effects on another type, but differences in positive effects can be substantial and need to be taken into account when we design educational environments. Thus we pay considerable attention to the 'learning history' of students, how they have progressed academically, how they feel about themselves, their cognitive and personality development, and their social skills and attitudes.

Also students will change as their repertoire of learning strategies increases. As they become a more powerful learning community, they will be able to accomplish more and more types of learning more effectively. In a very real sense, increasing aptitude to learn is the fundamental purpose of models of teaching.

Debates about educational method have seemed to imply that schools and teachers should choose one approach over another. However, it is far more likely that for optimum opportunity to learn, students need a range of instructional approaches drawn from the information processing, social, personal and behavioural families.

3 Learning to think inductively

Thinking inductively is inborn and lawful. This is revolutionary work, because schools have decided to teach in a lawless fashion, subverting inborn capacity.

Hilda Taba to a group sitting on the steps of the Lincoln Memorial, 1966

The 'inductive model' is our first example from the information processing family. In the following scenarios the five teachers are using almost the same process with content from several curriculum areas and with primary and secondary school children. In each case, the process objectives (learning to build, test and use categories) are combined with the content objectives (inquiring into and mastering important topics in the curriculum).

SCENARIO I

At the Motilal Nehru School of Sports in the state of Haryana, India, two groups of 15-year-olds are engaged in the study of a botany unit that focuses on the structure of plant life. One group is studying the textbook with the tutorial help of their instructor, who illustrates the structures with plants found in the grounds of the school. We will call this group the presentation/illustration group. The other group, which we will call the inductive group, is taught by Bharati Baveja, an instructor at Delhi University. This group is presented with a large number of labelled plants. Working in pairs, Bharati's students build classifications of the plants based on the structural characteristics of their roots, stems and leaves. Periodically the pairs share their classifications and generate labels for them.

Occasionally Mrs Baveja employs concept attainment to introduce a concept designed to expand the students' frame of reference and induce more complex classification. She also supplies the scientific names for the categories the students invent. Eventually Mrs Baveja presents the students with some new specimens and asks them to see if they can predict the structure of one part of the plant from the observation of another part (as predicting the root structure from the observation of the leaves). Finally she asks them to collect some more specimens and fit them to the categories they have developed so they can determine how comprehensive their categories have become. They discover that most of the new plants will fit into existing categories but that new categories have to be invented to hold some of them.

After two weeks of study, the two groups take a test over the content of the unit and are asked to analyse more specimens and name their structural characteristics.

The inductive group has gained twice as much on the test of knowledge and can correctly identify the structure of eight times more specimens than the presentation/illustration group.

SCENARIO 2

Jack Wilson is a Year 2 teacher in Cambridge, England. He meets daily for reading instruction with a group of children who are progressing quite well. He is concerned, however, that they have trouble dealing with new words unless they are able to figure out the meaning from context. If they are able to figure out what the word means from the rest of the sentence, they seem to have no difficulty using principles they have learned to sound the words out. He has concluded that they don't have full control over phonetic and structural analysis concepts and principles. He plans the following activity, which is designed to help them develop concepts of how words are structured and to use that knowledge in tackling words unknown to them.

Jack prepares a deck of cards with one word on each card. He selects words with particular prefixes and suffixes, and he deliberately puts in words that have the same root words but different prefixes and suffixes. He picks prefixes and suffixes because they are very prominent structural characteristics of words – very easy to identify. (He will later proceed to more subtle phonetic and structural features.) Jack plans a series of learning activities over the next several weeks using the deck of cards as a data base. Here are some of the words:

| set | reset | heat | preheat | plant | replan |
| run | rerun | set | preset | plan | preplan |

When the group of children arrives on Monday morning, Jack gives several cards to each child. He keeps the remainder, counting on gradually increasing the amount of information children get. Jack asks each child to read a word on one of the cards and describe something about the word. Other children can add to the description. In this way the structural properties of the word are brought to the children's attention. The discussion brings to light features like initial consonants (begins with an *s*, vowels, pairs of consonants (*pl*), and so on).

After the children have familiarized themselves with the assortment of words, Jack asks them to put the words into groups. 'Put the words that go together in piles', he instructs. The children begin studying their cards, passing them back and forth as they sort out the commonalities. At first their card groups reflected only the initial letters or the meanings of the words, such as whether they referred to motion or warmth. Gradually they noticed the prefixes, how they were spelled, and looked up their meanings in the dictionary, discovering how the addition of the prefixes affected the meanings of the root words.

When the children finished sorting the words, Jack asked them to talk about each category, telling what the cards had in common. Gradually, because of the way Jack had selected the data, the children could discover the major prefixes and suffixes and reflect on their meaning. Then he gave them sentences in which words not in their deck began and ended with those prefixes and suffixes and asked them to figure out the meanings of those words, applying the concepts they had formed to help them unlock these meanings.

By selecting different sets of words, Jack led the class through the categories of consonant and vowel sounds and structures they would need to deal with unfamiliar words, providing the children with many opportunities to practise inductive learning. Jack studies their progress and adjusts the classification tasks to lead them to a thorough understanding and the ability to use their new knowledge to tackle unfamiliar words.

SCENARIO 3

Eight-year-old Seamus is apparently playing in his kitchen. In front of him are a number of plates. On one is a potato, cut in quarters. Another contains an apple, similarly cut. The others contain a variety of fruits and vegetables. Seamus pushes into the segments of potato a number of copper and zinc plates which are wired together and to a tiny light bulb. He nods with satisfaction when the bulb begins to glow. He disconnects the bulb, attaches a voltmeter, examines it briefly and then reattaches the bulb. He repeats the process with the apple, examining the bulb and voltmeter once again. Then come the raspberries, lemon, carrot and so on. His father enters the room and Seamus looks up. 'I was right about the raspberries,' he says, 'we can use them as in a battery. But some of these other things . . .'

Seamus is, of course, classifying fruits and vegetables in terms of whether they can interact with metals to produce electric current.

SCENARIO 4

Diane Scott provided her first grade children with sets of tulip bulbs which they classified. They formed groups according to size, whether two were joined together ('Some have babies on them'), whether they had 'coats', or whether they had the beginnings of what look like roots. Now the children are planting their bulbs, trying to find out whether the variation in attributes they identified will affect how the tulips grow. ('Will the big ones [bulbs] grow bigger?' 'Will the babies grow on their own?', etc.) She has designed the science curriculum area around the basic processes of building categories, making predictions and testing their validity.

SCENARIO 5

Dr Makibbin's social studies class is examining data from a large demographic base on the nations of the world. One group of students is looking at the base on Africa, another is studying Latin America, and the others are poring over the data from Asia and Europe. They are searching for correlations among variables, such as trying to learn whether *per capita* income is associated with life expectancy and whether educational level is associated with rate of increase in population and so on. As they share the results of their inquiry, they will compare the continents, trying to learn whether the correlations within each are comparable to the others.

INDUCTIVE THINKING AS A MODEL OF LEARNING AND TEACHING

The five scenarios that introduce this chapter illustrate the inductive model in operation. As with the other more powerful and utilitarian models of teaching, the inductive model has a long history. Inductive thinking has been written about since the classical Greek period, and the model has been polished and studied formally during the last 30 years. Very important to current classroom use was the work of Hilda Taba (1966, 1967), who was largely responsible for popularizing the term *teaching strategy* and for shaping the inductive model so that it could be conveniently used to design curricula and lessons.

The inductive model causes students to collect information and examine it closely, to organize it into concepts and to learn to manipulate those concepts. Used regularly, this strategy increases students' abilities to form concepts efficiently and increases the range of perspectives from which they can view information.

If a group of students regularly engage in inductive activity, the group can be taught to use increasing numbers of sources of data. The students can learn to examine data from many sides and to scrutinize all aspects of objects and events. For example, imagine students studying communities. We can expect that at first their data will be superficial, but their increasingly sophisticated inquiry will turn up more and more attributes that they can use for classifying the information they are gathering. Also if a classroom of students works in groups to form concepts and data, and then the groups share the categories they develop, they will stimulate each other to look at the information from different perspectives.

PHASES OF THE MODEL

Think about the scenarios at the beginning of the chapter as you review the phases of the inductive model of teaching and learning. The phases of the inductive model include:

1 collection and presentation of the data that are relevant to a topic or
   problem;
2 examining and enumerating the data into categories whose members
   have common attributes;
3 classifying the data and developing labels for the categories so that
   they can be manipulated symbolically; and
4 converting the categories into hypotheses or skills.

The inductive model has a rolling structure that evolves over time;
inductive inquiries are rarely brief. The essence of the inductive process
is the continual collecting and sifting of information, the construction
of ideas (particularly categories) that provide conceptual control over
territories of information, the generation of hypotheses to be explored
in an effort to understand relationships better or provide solutions to
problems, and the conversion of knowledge into skills that have practical application.

The data collection and presentation phase

Inductive operations involve organizing data and pulling it apart and
reorganizing it in the search for ideas. Thus collecting data occurs
early, but new data may be added or discarded as an inquiry proceeds.
While teaching students to work inductively we often present sets of
otherwise unorganized data to the students, and we will always do so on
occasions when we want to select the substance for their initial inquiry.
However, we will teach them to collect data and create data sets, and
many inductive inquiries begin with a collection phase. Data sets are
developed from substantive domains that are identified for academic
purposes. Domains are arbitrary boundaries for study and are quite
various – they are territories to be explored. They can be defined geo-
graphically ('Let's study everything in the town centre') or by general
categories (the economic systems of all nations, or the nations of Asia,
poems written last year by Chinese women), and are selected for the
reason that we believe it will be productive to study them. They need to
be significant by some academic standard. Although trivial things *can*
be studied and classified, we usually do not spend valuable curricular
time on them. However, serious inquiry can turn the apparently trivial
into something quite significant. Irving Goffman's (1982) book *Gender
Advertisements* explores how images are formed in our public mind.
George Gerbner's (1974) studies of how print and film media shape
views of teachers is another.

The phase of examining and enumerating data

The data need to be examined closely, whether rocks or poems or
philosophies, and labelled or tagged so we can identify them as we
move them around. Rocks can have numbers or tags of different
colours; poems have names and can have numbers as well; philosophies

can be named after the philosophers. Items in the data set also need to be studied very carefully so that their attributes are teased out richly. This phase needs to be done carefully or the inquiry will be superficial. We have found that many teachers tend to rush this phase, which is almost always a mistake.

The first phase of classifying

To be really productive we generally classify data several times. The first phase is important, but we have a tendency to classify on gross characteristics and just one or two attributes, to confine ourselves to one-way classifications. When classifying poems we rely on the more obvious differences in subject matter, mood and device. In doing this we are just getting started. However, the first pass at building and sharing categories gets us going.

Sometimes after the first exercise in classification we find we want to add some more data to our set or that we are seeing things we didn't pay attention to when we were studying and enumerating the data. In those cases we go back and collect or examine again, or both.

The further phases of classifying

Digging into our data again, we reclassify, refine or collapse categories, experiment with two- and three-way schemes, and categories emerge and are shared. We gradually get control of our data.

Sometimes we alternate classification with a further search for data.

The phase of building hypotheses and generating skills

Just having categories is educative. When we classify character sketches drawn from novels and short stories, we discover ways that authors introduce characters knowing those ways enables us to read with a more refined eye. However, if we keep pushing at the categories, we can milk them for hypotheses and convert some of them into useful skills. Suppose we discovered that women writers used analogies more frequently than male writers when introducing characters: we might hypothesize that women would use analogies more in all phases of their writing. We can develop a new inquiry to test that hypothesis. If we pursue the subject, we can try to find out why.

Building skills from categories requires learning what to do to produce something that fits the category. Suppose for example, that we discover metaphors as a device used by our poets. If we want to produce metaphors we need to practise and to compare our products with the metaphors generated by expert writers.

Beside these four main phases, it is also important to consider how to engage students in inductive activities. Taba for example invented teaching moves in the form of tasks given to the students, and we follow her example. For instance, asking students to 'Look up the data on *per capita* income and population growth for 12 countries from each of the major regions of the world' will induce the students to create a data file. The task 'Decide which countries are most alike' is likely to cause people to group those things that have been listed. The question 'What would we call these groups?' begins a task likely to induce people to develop labels or categories. Asking the students to correlate income and growth leads to further interpretation and the development of hypotheses (they will find that there is an inverse correlation between *per capita* income and population growth and wonder why). An example of the development of skill is where students have classified ways that authors introduce characters and then experiment with those classifications, learning multiple ways *they* can introduce characters.

The teacher moves the model along by means of eliciting questions to guide the student from one phase of activity into the next – at the appropriate time. For example, the grouping of data would be premature if the data had not been identified and enumerated. But to delay too long before moving into the next phase would be to lose opportunities for learning and could decrease students' cognitive interest.

To teach students to respond to the model, we advise teachers to begin by leading the students through activities based on data sets that are presented to them, and in later lessons to teach students how to create and organize data sets.

RESEARCH

Although much research on information processing models has been focused on how to increase students' ability to form and use concepts and hypotheses, a number of questions asked by both practitioners and laymen are particularly relevant here. The questions mainly reflect a concern that a concentration on thinking might inhibit the mastery of content.

Teachers put the question something like this: 'I have much content to cover. If I devote energy to the teaching of thinking, won't the students miss out on the basic skills and content that are the "core" of the curriculum?'

Several reviews of research have addressed this question. El-Nemr (1979) concentrated on the teaching of biology as inquiry in high schools and colleges. He looked at the effects on student achievement, on the development of process skills and on attitudes toward science. The experimentally orientated biology curricula achieved positive effects on all three outcomes. Bredderman's (1983) analysis included a broader range of science programmes and included the elementary grades. He also reported positive effects for information acquisition, creativity, science process and, in addition, on intelligence tests where they were included. Hillocks' (1987) review of the teaching of writing produced similar results. In short, the inductive inquiry-orientated approaches to the teaching of writing produced average effect sizes of about 0.60 compared to treatments that covered the same material, but without the inductive approaches to the teaching/learning process.

Some other researchers have approached the question of 'coverage' in terms of the transfer of the teaching of thinking from one curriculum to another, and found that inquiry-orientated curricula appear to stimulate growth in other, apparently unconnected, areas. For example, Smith's (1980) analysis of aesthetics curricula shows that the implementation of the arts-orientated curricula was accompanied by gains in the basic skills areas.

The question of time and efficiency has been addressed recently in a number of large scale field studies in the basic curriculum areas. An example has been provided by the 190 elementary school teachers of an Iowa school district. The teachers and administrators in this district focused on improving the quality of writing of their students by using the inductive model of teaching to help students explore the techniques used by published authors to accomplish such tasks as introducing characters, establishing settings and describing action. At intervals teachers collected samples of the children's writing, and those samples were scored by experts who did not know the identity of the children.

By the end of the year, student writing had improved dramatically. In the fourth grade for example, their end-of-year scores for writing quality were higher than the end-of-year scores for eighth grade students the previous year! Students had made greater gains in one year than were normally achieved by comparable students over a period of four years. Moreover, students at all levels of writing quality had gained substantially – from the ones who started with the poorest writing skills to the ones who began with the most developed skills. The 'gender gap' in writing (males often lag behind females in developing writing skills) narrowed significantly (Joyce *et al.* 1994, 1996).

That the same model of teaching reached all the students is surprising to many people but it is a typical finding in studies of teaching and teaching strategies. Teachers who reach the students with poor histories of learning and help them out of their rut also propel the best students into higher states of growth than they have been accustomed to.

REFLECTIONS

The inductive model of learning and teaching is designed to instruct students in concept formation and, simultaneously, to teach concepts, and the application of concepts/generalizations. It nurtures attention to logic, attention to language and the meaning of words, and attention to the nature of knowledge. Figure 3.1 displays the instructional and nurturant effects of the inductive thinking model, and Table 3.1 the syntax of the model.

It is sometimes thought that higher order thinking is reserved for the mature. Not so. *Students of all ages can process information richly.* Although

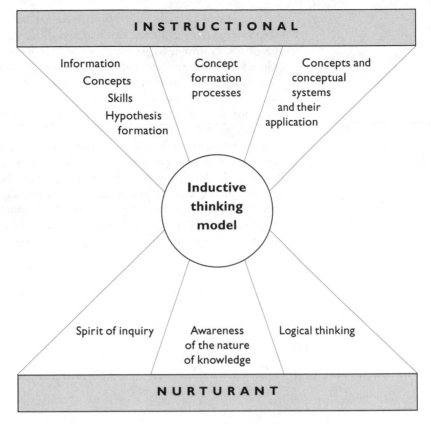

Figure 3.1 Instructional and nurturant effects of the inductive thinking model

Table 3.1 Syntax of the inductive model of learning and teaching

Phase 1: data collection/presentation
Identifying and enumerating the data relevant to a topic or problem.

Phase 2: examining and enumerating data
Grouping individual data or items into categories that have common
    attributes.

Phase 3: classifying data and labelling
Interpreting the data and developing labels for the categories. This also
    involves identifying and exploring critical relationships and making
    inferences so that they can be manipulated symbolically.

Phase 4: creating hypotheses and converting categories to skills
Predicting consequences and verifying the prediction.

the content of primary education needs to be replete with concrete experience, young children can learn to think well. In Hempshill Hall school for example, as we saw in the first scenario in the book, the inductive model was being used with Year 1 students to broaden their vocabulary and to develop phonological awareness. Similarly, complex inquiry-orientated models of instruction have turned out to be the best educational medicine for students who start school slowly or, later, have the poorest learning histories.

Old fencing masters used to tell their students that you grip the sword as you would hold a sparrow. If you hold it too tightly, it cannot breathe. If you hold it too loosely, it will fly away. Good thinking bears analogy to the fencer's grip, combining discipline with flexibility. If we are to help children become more powerful and flexible thinkers, we have to master the paradox and create environments that offer challenge and strong support without smothering the very characteristics we seek to nurture.

4 Learning to explore concepts

What that kid did made the point so everybody could hear it. Four times last week he was in concept attainment lessons taught by the student teachers. So he said we owed him one. If we'd get him some second graders to teach, he'd make a data set and teach the same kind of lesson. And he wanted to be videotaped like the student teachers were. So we got him the kids and he taught the lesson and he did a great job. So now everybody understands that the whole point is to teach the kids the model, and practice will do it.

Kay Vandergrift to Bruce Joyce, November 1969

'Concept attainment' is our second model from the information processing family. In the following two examples the teachers are helping their students to categorize, to learn concepts and to study how they think.

SCENARIO I

We happen on a classroom in Hong Kong. Dr Ora Kwo is teaching a lesson on English to her students. She has a chart in the front of the room. We will follow her as she leads her students through an exercise that employs it. There are two headings on the chart:

Positive exemplars   Negative exemplars

She puts the following two words under the headings:

clean   help

'Take a look at these two words. How are they alike and how are they different? *Clean* has the attributes of our category. *Help* does not.' She places cards containing two more words on the chart.

clear   trim

'Now examine this pair. *Clear* has the attributes we are concerned with. *Help* does not. What do *clear* and *clean* have in common that *help* and *trim* do not?'

She asks the students to work singly during this phase of the exercise. She presents two more words and asks the students to compare and contrast them, trying to discover what the positive exemplars have in common that they do not share with the negative exemplars.

clip   hip

'Now, what do you see? Please write down your hypothesis at this point. What do you think are the attributes that the *positive* words have in common that they do not share with the words I have identified as *negative*?' After a few seconds, she proceeds to the next pair of words.

clap   lap

'Did any of you have to change your ideas?' She looks around the room and finds that several did. Then, in the same fashion, she presents several other pairs of words:

cling   ring

climb   limb

club   tree

Ora continued until she had presented a dozen more pairs. Then she presented a word and asked the students whether they believed, on the basis of their hypothesis, that it was positive or negative.

lip

Thirty of the students correctly identified the word as a negative exemplar. Six did not. She inferred that the 30 were concentrating on the *cl* while the others were still not sure whether having either a *c* or an *l* would qualify it. Therefore she presented to them the following series:

clue   flue

clarify   rarefy

clack   lack

Then she asked the question again. 'What do you think of this one?'

crack

All the students identified the word as negative. Thus she presented the next one.

clank

They all identified it as positive. She proceeded to present them with a half-dozen positive and negative exemplars and, when they could identify them correctly, asked them to share their current hypotheses. ('The positives begin with *cl* and sound like [imagine the sound].') She had them identify what was *not* critical (meanings, endings, etc.) and then asked them how they would make negatives positive (transforming *an* to *clan* and so forth, until she was satisfied that the idea was clear).

Ora then sent them to scour a couple of stories, looking for positive exemplars, and gave them a list of words to classify on the basis of the attributes of the category.

We have, of course, looked in on a phonics lesson for students for whom English is a second language. The lesson is designed with the concept attainment model of teaching and teaches concepts useful in both writing and spelling.

SCENARIO 2

Mrs Stern's eighth grade class in Houston, Texas, has been studying the characteristics of the 14 largest cities in the United States. They have collected data on size, ethnicity of population, types of industry, location and proximity to natural resources.

Working in groups, the students have collected information and summarized it on a series of charts now pasted up around the room. One Wednesday in November, Mrs Stern says 'Today, let's try a series of exercises designed to help us understand these cities better. I have identified a number of concepts that help us compare and contrast them. I am going to label our charts either *yes* or *no*. If you look at the information we have and think about the populations and the other characteristics, you will identify the ideas that I have in mind. I'm going to start with the city that's a *yes* and then one that's a *no*, and so forth. Think about what the *yeses* have in common. Then write down after the second *yes* the idea that you think connects those two places and keep testing those ideas as we go along. Let's begin with our own city', she says. 'Houston is a *yes*.'

The students look at the information about Houston: its size, industries, location, ethnic composition. Then Mrs Stern points to Baltimore, Maryland.

'Baltimore is a *no*', she says. Then she points to San Jose, California. 'Here is another *yes*', she comments.

The students look for a moment at the information about San Jose. Two or three raise their hands.

'I think I know what it is', one offers.

'Hold on to your idea', she replies. 'See if you're right.' She then selects another *yes* – Seattle, Washington; then Detroit, Michigan, is a *no*; then Miami, Florida, is a *yes*. After each city is presented, she allows students time to study their information. She continues until all students think they know what the concept is, and then they begin to share concepts.

'What do you think it is, Jill?'

'The *yeses* all have mild climates', says Jill. 'That is, it doesn't get very cold in any of them.'

'It gets pretty cold in Salt Lake City', objects another.

'Yes, but not as cold as in Chicago, Detroit or Baltimore', another student counters.

'I think the *yeses* are all rapidly growing cities. Each one of them increased more than 10 per cent during the last ten years.' There is some student discussion about whether this is accurate.

'All the *yeses* have lots of different industries', volunteers another.

'That's true, but almost all of these cities do', replies another student.

Finally, the students decide the *yeses* are all cities that are growing very fast and have relatively mild climates.

'That's right', agrees Mrs Stern. 'That's exactly what I had in mind. Now let's do this again. This time I want to begin with Baltimore, Maryland, and now it is a *yes*.'

The exercise is repeated several times. Students learn that Mrs Stern has grouped the cities on the basis of their relationship to waterways, natural resources, ethnic composition and several other dimensions.

The students are beginning to see patterns in their data. Finally Mrs Stern says 'Now, each of you try to group the cities in a way that you think is important. Then take turns and lead us through this exercise, helping us to see which ones you place in which category. Then we'll discuss the ways we can look at cities and how we can use different categories for different purposes. Finally, we'll use the inductive model and you can see how many relationships you can find.'

CONCEPT ATTAINMENT AS A MODEL OF LEARNING AND TEACHING

Concept attainment is 'the search for and listing of attributes that can be used to distinguish exemplars from nonexemplars of various categories' (Bruner *et al.* 1967: 233). Whereas *concept formation*, which is the basis of the inductive model described in the previous chapter, requires the students to decide the basis on which they will build categories, concept attainment requires a student to figure out the attributes of a category that is already formed in another person's mind by comparing and contrasting examples (called exemplars) that contain the characteristics (called attributes) of the concept with examples that do not contain those attributes.

To create such lessons, we need to have our category clearly in mind. As an example, let us consider the concept *adjective*. Adjectives are words, so we select some words that are adjectives (these become the positive exemplars) and some that are not (these become negative exemplars – the ones that do not have the attributes of the category *adjective*). We present the words to the students in pairs. Consider the following four pairs:

triumphant	triumph
large	chair
broken	laugh
painful	pain

It is probably best to present the words in sentences to provide more information, because adjectives function in the context of a sentence. For example:

Yes: Our *triumphant* team returned home after winning the state championship.
No: After his *triumph*, Senator Jones gave a gracious speech.
Yes: The *large* truck backed slowly into the barn.
No: He sank gratefully into the *chair*.
Yes: The *broken* arm healed slowly.
No: His *laugh* filled the room.
Yes: The *painful* separation had to be endured.

No: He felt a sharp *pain* in his ankle.

To carry on the model, we need about 20 pairs in all – we would need more pairs of positive and negative exemplars if the concept were more complex than our current example, *adjectives*.

We begin the process by asking the students to scrutinize the sentences and to pay particular attention to the words in italics. Then we instruct them to compare and contrast the functions of the positive and negative exemplars. 'The positive exemplars have something in common in the work they do in the sentence. The negative exemplars do different work.'

We ask the students to make notes about what they believe the exemplars have in common. Then we present more sets of exemplars and ask them whether they still have the same idea. If not, we ask what they now think. We continue to present exemplars until most of the students have an idea they think will withstand scrutiny. At that point, we ask one of the students to share his or her idea and how he or she arrived at it. One possible response is as follows: 'Well, at first I thought that the positive words were longer. Then some of the negatives were longer, so I gave that up. Now, I think that the positive ones always come next to some other word and do something to it. I'm not sure just what.'

Then other students share their ideas. We provide some more examples. Gradually, the students agree that each positive exemplar adds something to the meaning of a word that stands for an object or a person, or qualifies it in some way.

We continue by providing some more sentences and by asking the students to identify the words that belong to our concept. When they can do that, we provide them with the name of the concept (*adjective*) and ask them to agree on a definition.

The final activity is to ask the students to describe their thinking as they arrived at the concepts and to share how they used the information that was given.

For homework, we ask the students to find adjectives in a short story we assign them to read. We will examine the exemplars they come up with to be sure that they have a clear picture of the concept.

This process ensures that the students learn the attributes that define a concept (the defining attributes) and can distinguish those from other important attributes that do not form the definition. All the words, for example, are composed of letters, but the presence of letters does not define the part of speech. Letters are important characteristics of all items in the data set, but are not critical in defining the category we call *adjective*. The students learn that it is the function of the word that is the essence of the concept, not what it denotes. *Pain* and *painful* both refer to trauma, but only one is an adjective.

As we teach students with this method, we help them become more efficient in attaining concepts. They learn the rules of the model.

Let us look at another example, this time language study for beginning readers.

Teacher [presents 6-year-old children with the following list of words labelled *yes* or *no*]:

fat (Yes)	fate (No)
mat (Yes)	mate (No)
rat (Yes)	rate (No)

'I have a list of words here. Notice that some have *yes* by them and some have *no* by them. [Children observe and comment on the format. Teacher puts the list aside for a moment.] Now, I have an idea in my head and I want you to try to guess what I'm thinking of. Remember the list I showed you. [Picks up the list.] This will help you guess my idea because each of these is a clue. The clues work this way: if a word has a *yes* by it [points to first word], then it is an example of what I'm thinking. If it has a *no* by it, then it is not an example.'

[The teacher continues to work with the children so that they understand the procedures of the lesson and then turns over the task of working out the concept to them.]

Teacher: 'Can you come up with a name for my idea? Do you know what my idea is?' [The children decide what they think the teacher's idea is. She continues the lesson.]

Teacher: 'Let's see if your idea is correct by testing it. I'll give you some examples, and you tell me if they are a *yes* or a *no*, based on your idea.' [She gives them more examples. This time the children supply the *noes* and *yeses*.]

kite (No)	cat (Yes)
hat (Yes)	hate (No)

'Well, you seem to have it. Now think up some words you believe are *yeses*. The rest of us will tell you whether your example is right. You tell us if we guessed correctly.' [The exercise ends with the children generating their own examples and telling how they arrived at the concept.]

In this lesson, if the children simply identified the concept as the *at* vowel-consonant phonogram and correctly recognized *cat* and *hat* as a *yes*, they have attained the concept on a simple level. If they verbalized the distinguishing features (essential attributes) of the *at* sound, they attained the concept on a more advanced level. There are different levels of attainment: correctly distinguishing examples from non-examples is easier than verbalizing the attributes of the concept. Students will probably be able to distinguish examples correctly before they will be able to explain verbally either the concept name or its essential characteristics.

We have used terms such as *exemplar* and *attribute* to describe categorizing activity and concept attainment. Derived from Bruner's study (Bruner *et al.* 1967) of concepts and how people attain them, each term has a special meaning and function in all forms of conceptual learning, especially concept attainment.

Exemplars. The exemplars are a subset of a collection of data or a data set. The category is the subset or collection of samples that share one or more characteristics that are missing in the others. It is by comparing the positive exemplars and contrasting them with the negative ones that the concept or category is learned.

Attributes. All items of data have features and we refer to these as *attributes.* Nations, for example, have areas with agreed-on boundaries, people and governments that can deal with other nations. Cities have boundaries, people and governments also, but they cannot independently deal with other countries. Distinguishing nations from cities depends on locating the attribute of international relations.

Essential attributes are those that are critical to the domain under consideration. Exemplars of a category have many other attributes that may not be relevant to the category itself. For example, nations have trees and flowers also, but these are not relevant to the definition of nation; although they, too, represent important domains and can also be categorized and subcategorized. However, with respect to the category *nation*, trees and flowers are not essential.

Once a category is established, it is named so that we can refer to it symbolically. As the students name the categories, they should do so in terms of attributes. Thus in the scenario at the very beginning of the chapter, they will describe the category as words beginning with *cl* and sounding like (imagine the sound of *cl* at the beginning of a word). Then if there is a technical term (*adjective* in one of the other examples above), we supply it. However, the concept attainment process is not one of guessing names. It is used to get the attributes of a category clear. Then the name can be created or supplied. Thus the name is merely the term given to a category. *Fruit, dog, government, ghetto* are all names given to a class of experiences, objects, configurations or processes. Although the items commonly grouped together in a single category may differ from one another in certain respects (dogs, for example, vary greatly), the common features cause them to be referred to by the same general term.

Often we teach ideas that students already know intuitively without knowing the name itself. For instance, young children often put pictures of fruit together for the reason that they are 'all things you can eat'. They are using one characteristic to describe the concept instead of the name or label. If students know a concept, however, they can easily learn the name for it and their verbal expressions will be more articulate. Part of knowing a concept is recognizing positive instances of it and also distinguishing closely related, but negative, examples. Just knowing terms will not suffice for this. Many people know the terms *metaphor* and *simile* but have never clarified the attributes of each well enough to tell them apart or apply them in their own writing. One cannot knowingly employ metaphoric language without a clear understanding of its attributes.

Multiple attributes are another consideration in clarifying concepts. Concepts range from cases in which the mere presence of a single attribute is sufficient for membership in a category to those in which the presence of several attributes is necessary. Membership in the category *boy* requires maleness and youth. Membership in the category *red-haired boy* requires the presence of maleness, youth and red hair. *Intelligent, gregarious, athletic red-haired boys* is a concept that requires the presence of several attributes simultaneously.

In literature, social studies and science we deal with numerous concepts that are defined by the presence of multiple attributes, and sometimes attribute value is a consideration also. Consider the theatrical concept *romantic comedy*. A positive example must be a play or film, must have enough humorous values to qualify as a comedy, and must be romantic as well. Negative exemplars include plays that are neither funny nor romantic, are funny but not romantic, and are romantic but not funny.

To teach a concept we have to be very clear about its defining attributes and about whether attribute values are a consideration. We must also select our negative exemplars so that items with some but not all the attributes can be ruled out.

PHASES OF THE MODEL

Let's look briefly at the three phases of instruction that work together to form a fully articulated concept attainment lesson. Think about the scenarios and examples presented above as you read the description of each phase.

Phase 1 involves presenting data to the learner. Each unit of data is a separate example or nonexample of the concept. The units are presented in pairs. The data may be events, people, objects, stories, pictures, or any other differentiable units. The learners are informed that there is one idea that all the positive examples have in common; their task is to develop a hypothesis about the nature of the concept. The instances are presented in a prearranged order and are labelled *yes* or *no*. Learners are asked to compare and justify the attributes of the different examples. (The teacher or students may want to maintain a record of the attributes.) Finally they are asked to name their concepts and state the rules or definitions of the concepts according to their essential attributes. (Their hypotheses are not confirmed until the next phase; students may not know the names of some concepts, but the names can be provided when the concepts are confirmed.)

In *Phase 2*, the students test their attainment (or understanding) of the concept, first by correctly identifying additional unlabelled examples of the concept and then by generating their own examples. After this, the teacher (and students) confirm or refute their original hypotheses, revising their choice of concepts or attributes as necessary.

In *Phase 3*, students begin to analyse the strategies by which they attain concepts. As we have indicated, some learners initially try broad constructs and gradually narrow the field; others begin with more discrete constructs. The learners can describe their patterns; whether they focused on attributes or concepts, whether they did so one at a time or several at once, and what happened when their hypotheses were not confirmed. Did they change strategies? Gradually, they can compare the effectiveness of different strategies.

RESEARCH

Tennyson and Cocchiarella (1986) have conducted important research into concept learning. In the course of their explorations they have dealt with a number of questions that can help us design concept courses, units and lessons with concept attainment. They have compared treatments where students induce attributes and definitions, in the same way that we have been describing the process and treatments where the definition is discussed before the list of exemplars is presented. In both types of treatment, the students developed clearer concepts and retained them longer when the examination of the exemplars *preceded* the discussion of attributes and definitions. Tennyson and Cocchiarella also discovered that the first positive exemplars presented should be the *clearest possible prototypes*, especially with multiple-attribute concepts. In other words, the teacher should not try to 'fake out' the students with vague exemplars, but should take care to facilitate concept learning by arranging the data sets so that students deal with less-clear exemplars in the phases where the principles are applied.

Tennyson and Cocchiarella have also concluded that students develop procedural knowledge (how to attain concepts) with practice, and that the more procedural knowledge the students possess, the more effectively they attain and can apply conceptual knowledge. Like the research of McKinney *et al.* (1983), their work has convinced them that teaching with concept attainment procedures is far more efficient for student learning than presenting students with the names of concepts, definitions and illustrations, a common variant of the familiar recitation method of teaching.

REFLECTIONS

Concept teaching provides a chance to analyse the students' thinking processes and to help them develop more effective strategies. The approach can involve various degrees of student participation and student control, and materials of varying complexity.

Teaching students to explore concepts can accomplish several learning goals. While concept attainment strategies are designed for instruction on specific concepts and on concepts in general, they also provide practice in inductive reasoning and opportunities for altering and improving students' concept building strategies. Finally, especially with abstract concepts, the strategies nurture an awareness of alternative perspectives, a sensitivity to logical reasoning in communication and a tolerance of ambiguity. In Hempshill Hall school, teachers made clear in their schemes of work the distinction between the inductive and

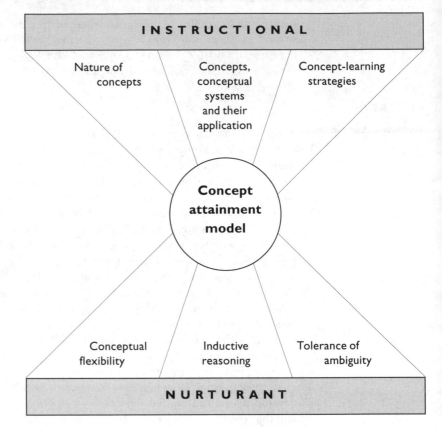

Figure 4.1 Instructional and nurturant effects of the concept attainment model

Table 4.1 Syntax of the concept attainment model of learning and teaching

Phase 1: presentation of data and identification of the concept
The teacher presents labelled examples.
Students compare attributes in positive and negative examples.
Students generate and test hypotheses.
Students state a definition according to the essential attributes.

Phase 2: testing attainment of the concept
Students identify additional unlabelled examples as *yes* or *no*.
The teacher confirms hypotheses, names concept and restates definitions
    according to essential attributes.
Students generate examples.

Phase 3: analysis of thinking strategies
Students describe thoughts.
Students discuss role of hypotheses and attributes.
Students discuss type and number of hypotheses.

concept formation models. As a general rule they also tried not to present facts or concepts to their pupils without using the phases of the concept model in their curriculum planning and classroom practice. Figure 4.1 displays the instructional and nurturant effects of concept attainment as a model of learning and teaching; Table 4.1 shows its syntax.

5 Learning to think metaphorically

Of all the models, synectics has got to give the most immediate pleasure when you're leading the exercises. We've been teaching kids (both elementary and secondary) to lead synectics. I have to admit that I always have a little touch of green when I turn it over to them, because they're going to have the fun, now.

Letter from Bruce Joyce to Bill Gordon, January 1971

Synectics is our third representative of the information processing family. As a model of learning, synectics teaches metaphoric thinking, and as is seen in the following examples, encourages students to generate new and creative ideas.

SCENARIO I

A secondary school class is creating a book of short stories and poems. Their English teacher, Peter Brown, has gradually become aware that some stories and many of the poems are hackneyed and ordinary. He has been helping individuals rewrite their poems and stories, and some of them have been improved, but on the whole he is disappointed with the work.

Then Brown runs across the work of William Gordon, who believes that creativity can be enhanced by a series of group exercises. These exercises are designed to help us understand the process of creativity more completely and to use new metaphors and analogies, to 'break set' and generate new alternatives. Brown decides to try Gordon's methods. One morning, he has each of his students read a poem and a short story. He then says, 'Today we're going to try something new that I hope will help us see our stories and poems in a different light. For the next 15 or 20 minutes, I want us to play with ideas and then have you go back to your work and see what you can do to improve it. At the end of this exercise, I'm going to ask you to rewrite part or all of your poems and stories.' He begins by asking what a poem is. The children give a variety of answers, from which Brown selects key words and writes them on the board.

'It doesn't have to rhyme.'

'It lets your feelings come out.'

'It uses different kinds of words.'

He then asks, 'How is a poem like a car?' The children are puzzled. Then one ventures, 'It takes you on a trip. It's a word trip and you have to have the road in your imagination.'

Someone else observes, 'It is self-propelled – you just get in it and it goes.'

Another student comments, 'When you're writing one, sometimes you have trouble getting the motor started.'

After a time, Brown says, 'Pick an animal – any animal.'

'How about a giraffe?' someone suggests.

'OK.' Then the teacher asks, 'How is a poem like a giraffe?'

'It has a lot of parts fastened together in funny ways', one student laughs.

'It kind of stands above everything else and looks at things in a different way', another adds.

The exercise goes on. After a time, Brown asks the students to select one of the words that they have dealt with in discussing a poem. They select the word *above*.

'How does it feel,' he asks, 'to be above?'

'You feel different', replies one. 'You can see things you don't ordinarily even notice', says another.

'You'll start feeling superior if you don't watch out', says a third student.

And so it goes. Finally, Brown asks the students to make lists of words they have been dealing with that seem to be opposite in some fashion – words that apply tension to each other. The students pick *giraffe* and *snail*, for they feel that both are animals but that they are very different in the way they live and move.

'Well,' Brown says, 'let's come back to your poems and short stories. Think of them as giraffes and snails together; write your poems or stories as if they were a giraffe and a snail holding hands, going through the woods together.'

Here are two products of that exercise.

The Great King

The great king stares out over his kingdom watching admiringly. The king stares out over his subjects, the sea gulls, fish, crabs, and everything else in the safe underwater home of his bottomless stomach. He lets out another breeze of his salty breath that can be smelled miles away. Another crash of his arm pushes away the sand to make damp mud that seagulls love. His ever stretching body wraps around the world of his presence for he is king of earth. He opens his heart to the people who take meaningful walks on his beach as if paying gratitude for everything he has done. Another crash sends a sea gull flying as if he was a royal messenger. The Ocean, the king, stares and is proud of what he sees.

The Motorcycle

It sounds like an enraged mountain lion.
It looks like a steel horse.
It shifts gears and changes notes.
It goes very fast.
The sound of the motorcycle
    breaks the stillness
        of the night.

Peter Brown has introduced metaphoric thinking to his students.

SCENARIO 2

Let us consider another example from Peter Brown's classroom.

Now Peter Brown's Year 9 class, which we met earlier, is preparing a campaign in opposition to a change in local government regulations that would permit a large grove of oak trees to be cut down as part of a large road building operation. They have made posters that they intend to display around their community and send to local and national politicians. They have the rough sketches for the posters and their captions, and they are examining them . . .

'Well, what do you think?' asks Gemma.

'Well, they're OK', says Tommy. 'They certainly say where we stand. Actually, though, I think they're a bit dull.'

'So do I', adds Holly. 'A couple of them are OK, but the others are really boring.'

'There's nothing really wrong with them,' chimes in another, 'they're just not very exciting.'

After some discussion, it is obvious that nearly everybody feels the same way. They decide that two or three of the posters are well designed and convey their message, but they need some others that would be more poignant.

'Let's try synectics', suggests one of the children.

'With pictures and captions?' asks one of the other children. 'I thought we could only use synectics with poetry. Can we use synectics with stuff like this?'

'Of course we can', says Gemma. 'I don't know why I didn't think of it. We've been doing it with poetry all year long.'

'Well I guess we've nothing to lose', adds Tommy. 'How would it work?'

'Well,' says Gemma, 'we could see these posters we've done as the beginning point and then go through a synectics training exercise and see if it gives us some ideas for pictures and captions. We could think of oak trees in terms of various personal and direct analogies and compressed conflicts.'

'Well let's try it', chimes in George.

'Let's start right now', says Sally. 'We could go through our exercises and then have lunchtime to think about the posters.'

'Can I be the leader?' asks Marsha. 'I've got some super ideas for some stretching exercises.'

'Is that OK?' says Gemma.

The children agree and Marsha begins.

'How is an oak tree like a toothpick?' she asks.

'You use the tree to pick the teeth of the gods', laughs George. Everyone joins in the laughter and they are off.

It's clear that Peter Brown has spent enough time using synectics that the students have internalized the process and purpose. They can proceed on their own, drawing on the model when they find it helpful.

SYNECTICS AS A MODEL OF LEARNING AND TEACHING

Synectics, designed by William J. J. Gordon and his associates (1961), is an interesting and delightful approach to the development of creative thinking. Gordon's initial work with synectics procedures was to develop 'creativity groups' within industrial organizations – that is, groups of persons trained to work together to function as problem solvers or product developers. Gordon has adapted synectics for use with schoolchildren, and materials containing many of the synectics activities are now being published. (For a complete list of synectics materials write to Synectics Education Systems, 121 Brattle Street, Cambridge, MA 02138, USA) The chief element in synectics is the use of analogies. In synectics exercises, students 'play' with analogies until they relax and begin to enjoy making more and more metaphoric comparisons, as did Brown's students. Then students use their analogies to tackle problems or formulate new ideas.

Ordinarily when we are confronted with a task – say a problem to be solved or a piece of writing to be produced – we consciously become logical. We prepare to write by making an outline of the points to be made. We analyse the elements of a problem and try to think it through. We use our existing storehouse of words and phrases to set down our ideas; we use our storehouse of learned solutions to face a problem.

For most problems and tasks of expressing ourselves, our logic works well enough. What do we do when our old solutions or ways of expressing ourselves are not sufficient to do the job? That is when we use synectics. This model of learning is designed to lead us into a slightly illogical world – to give us the opportunity to invent new ways of seeing things, expressing ourselves and approaching problems.

For example, teachers often struggle with the problem of how to deal with absenteeism. When a student repeatedly fails to come to school, what do they do? Frequently they turn to punishment. And what punishment is available? Frequently, suspension. That is logical, isn't it? To choose a severe punishment to match what is regarded as a severe infraction? The trouble with the solution is that it imposes on the student as a penalty exactly the same condition that the student had chosen in place of school. Synectics is used to help us develop fresh ways of thinking about the student, the student's motives, the nature of penalties, our goals and the nature of the problem. We have to develop empathy with someone who is in conflict with us. We have deliberately to avoid what appears to be logical thought because it leads us to an inadequate conception of the problem and thus an absurd (if logical) solution.

Through analogies we might conceive of our absentee as an 'unhappy lark', as on a 'destructive vacation', and the problem as one of ending an 'empty feast'. Our own needed behaviours may be ones of 'seductive strictness', 'strong lovingness', and 'dangerous peace-making'.

If we can relax the premises that have blocked us we can begin to generate new solutions. We can consider that we have been taking responsibility for the students in areas where they may need to be responsible for themselves. We can wonder whether the solution lies as much in our administration of the rules as it does in how we teach. We may wonder whether communities of peers might not create the energy and sense of belongingness that would attack the problem from a different perspective.

The social and scientific world in which we live abounds with problems for which new solutions are needed. Problems of poverty, international law, crime, just taxation, and war and peace would not exist if our logic did not fail us.

Striving for appropriate self-expression – trying to learn how to write and speak lucidly and compellingly – bedevils all of us. Two problems are persistent: grasping the subject clearly and comprehensively, and generating appropriate forms of expression.

Gordon grounds synectics in four ideas that challenge conventional views about creativity. First, creativity is important in everyday activities. Most of us associate the creative process with the development of great works of art or music, or perhaps with a clever new invention. Gordon emphasizes creativity as a part of our daily work and leisure lives. His model is designed to increase problem solving capacity, creative expression, empathy and insight into social relations. He also stresses that the meanings of ideas can be enhanced through creative activity by helping us see things more richly.

Second, the creative process is not at all mysterious. It can be described and it is possible to train persons directly to increase their creativity. Traditionally, creativity is viewed as a mysterious, innate and personal capacity that can be destroyed if its processes are probed too deeply. In contrast, Gordon believes that if individuals understand the basis of the creative process, they can learn to use that understanding to increase the creativity with which they live and work, independently and as members of groups. Gordon's view that creativity is enhanced by conscious analysis led him to describe it and create training procedures that can be applied in schools and other settings.

Third, creative invention is similar in all fields – the arts, the sciences, engineering – and is characterized by the same underlying intellectual processes. This idea is contrary to common belief. In fact, to many people, creativity is confined to the arts. In engineering and the sciences, however, it is simply called by another name: *invention*. Gordon maintains that the link between generative thinking in the arts and that in the sciences is quite strong.

Gordon's fourth assumption is that individual and group invention (creative thinking) are very similar. Individuals and groups generate ideas and products in much the same fashion. Again, this is very different from the stance that creativity is an intensely personal experience, not to be shared.

PHASES OF THE MODEL

Through the metaphoric activity of the synectics model, creativity becomes a conscious process. Metaphors establish a relationship of likeness, the comparison of one object or idea with another object or idea by using one in place of the other. Through these substitutions the creative process occurs, connecting the familiar with the unfamiliar or creating a new idea from familiar ideas.

In teaching persons to use synectics, three types of analogies are used as the basis of instructional exercises: personal analogy, direct analogy and compressed conflict.

To make *personal analogies* requires students to empathize with the ideas or objects to be compared. Students must feel they have become part of the physical elements of the problem. The identification may be with a person, plant, animal or nonliving thing. For example, students may be instructed, 'Be a car engine. What do you feel like? Describe how you feel when you are started in the morning; when your battery goes dead; when you come to a stop light.'

The emphasis in personal analogy is on empathetic involvement. Gordon gives the example of a problem situation in which the chemist personally identifies with the molecules in action. He might ask, 'How would I feel if I were a molecule?' and then feel himself being part of the 'stream of dancing molecules'.

Personal analogy requires loss of self as one transports oneself into another space or object.

Direct analogy is a simple comparison of two objects or concepts. The comparison does not have to be identical in all respects. Its function is simply to transpose the conditions of the real topic or problem situation to another situation in order to present a new view of an idea or problem. This involves identification with a person, plant, animal or nonliving thing. Gordon cites the experience of the engineer watching a shipworm tunnelling into a timber. As the worm ate its way into the timber by constructing a tube for itself and moving forward, the engineer Isambard Kingdom Brunel got the notion of using caissons to construct underwater tunnels (Gordon 1961: 40–1). Another example of direct analogy occurred when a group was attempting to devise a can with a top that could be used to cover the can once it had been opened.

In this instance, the analogy of the pea pod gradually emerged, which produced the idea of a seam placed a distance below the top of the can, thus permitting a removable lid.

The third metaphorical form is *compressed conflict*, generally a two-word description of an object in which the words seem to be opposites or to contradict each other. 'Tiredly aggressive' and 'friendly foe' are two examples. Gordon's examples are 'life-saving destroyer' and 'nourishing flame'. He also cites Pasteur's expression, 'safe attack'. Compressed conflicts, according to Gordon, provide the broadest insight into a new subject. They reflect the student's ability to incorporate two frames of reference with respect to a single object. The greater the distance between frames of reference, the greater the mental flexibility.

The following transcript of a synectics session in a US classroom shows a teacher helping students to see a familiar concept in fresh ways. At the beginning the students pick the concept of 'The Hood' (i.e. a gangster) to be described later in a writing composition. The lesson illustrates the six phases of the model (Gordon 1971: 7–11).

Phase I: description of present condition

Teacher: 'Now the problem is how to present this hood so that he's the hoodiest of hoods, but also a special, individualized person.'

The teacher asks students to discuss the familiar idea.

Student: 'He robs the Rabbinical School.'

Student: 'Let's name him.'

Student: 'Trog.'

Student: 'Al.'

Student: 'Slash.'

Student: 'Eric.'

Teacher: 'His names don't matter all that much. Let's call him Eric. What can we say about Eric?'

Student: 'Black, greasy hair. They all have black, greasy hair.'

Student: 'Long, blond hair – bleached – peroxided – with baby-blues. Eyes, I mean.'

Student: 'Bitten fingernails.'

Student: 'He's short and muscular.'

Student: 'Maybe he should be scrawny.'

Student: 'Bow-legged and yellow teeth and white, tight Levi's.'

Teacher: 'Is there anything here that's original? If you wrote that and backed off and read it, what would you think?' The teacher has students state the problem . . .

Class: 'No! Stereotyped! Standard! No personality! Very general! Same old stuff!'

Teacher: 'I agree. Eric, so far, is like every other hood. Now we have a problem to attack!'

Teacher: 'We must define a personality for this hood, for Eric, and define the task.'

Student: 'He's got to be individualized.'

Student: 'He has to have a way of getting money.'

Teacher: 'That's still an overgeneral idea of Eric. Let's put some strain into this idea. Hold it. Suppose I ask you to give me a direct analogy, something like Eric, but it's a machine. Tell me about a machine that has Eric's qualities as you see him. Not a human being, a machine.'

Phase 2: direct analogy

The teacher moves the students into analogies. He asks for a direct analogy. He also specifies the nature of the analogy – that is, a machine – in order to assure getting one of some distance (organic–inorganic comparison).

Student: 'He's a washing machine. A dishwasher.'

Student: 'An old beat-up car.'

Student: 'I want him to be a rich hood.'

Student: 'A beer factory.'

Student: 'A pinball machine in a dive.'

Student: 'Roulette.'

Teacher: 'You're focusing on the kinds of machines that Eric plays with. What is the thing that has his qualities in it?' The teacher reflects to students what they are doing so that they can be pushed to more creative analogies.

Student: 'An electric can opener.'

Student: 'A vacuum cleaner.'

Student: 'A neon sign.'

Student: 'A jello mould.'

Teacher: 'What is the machine that would make the strangest comparison between it and Eric? Go ahead and vote.' (The class voted for the dishwasher.) The teacher lets the students select the analogy to develop, but he provides the criterion for selection: 'strangest comparison'.

Teacher: 'First of all, how does a dishwasher work?' The teacher moves students simply to *explore* (describe) the machine they selected before making comparisons to their original source.

Student: 'People put in the dirty dishes and the water goes around and around and the dishes come out clean.'

Student: 'There's a blower in the one that's in the common room.'

Student: 'It's all steam inside. Hot!'

Student: 'I was thinking that if you want to make an analogy between the washer and the joy of dancing . . .'

Teacher: 'Hold it. Just stay with me. Don't look backward and make an analogical comparison too soon . . . and now is probably too soon.' The teacher controls responses to keep students from pushing to a comparison too soon. No comparisons to original source are made before moving on to another analogy.

Teacher: 'OK. Now, try being the dishwasher. What does it feel like to be a dishwasher? Tell us. Make yourself the dishwasher.'

Phase 3: personal analogy

The teacher asks for personal analogy.

Student: 'Well, all these things are given to me. Dishes are dirty. I want to get them clean. I'm trying. I throw off some steam and finally I get them clean. That's my duty.'

Teacher: 'Come on now people! You've got to put yourselves into the dishwasher and be it. All Lee's told us is what we already know about a dishwasher. There's none of *Lee* in it. It's hard, but try to *be* the dishwasher.' The teacher reflects to students the fact that they are describing the dishwasher, not what it *feels* like to be a dishwasher.

Student: 'It's very discouraging. You're washing all day long. I never get to know anybody. They keep throwing these dishes at me and I just throw the steam at them. I see the same type of dishes.'

Student: 'I get mad and get the dishes extra hot, and I burn people's fingers.'

Student: 'I feel very repressed. They keep feeding me dishes. All I can do is shut myself off.'

Student: 'I get so mad at everybody maybe I won't clean the dishes and then everybody will get sick.'

Student: 'I just love garbage. I want more and more. The stuff that falls off the dishes is soft and mushy and good to eat.'

Teacher: 'Let's look at the notes I've been making about your responses. Can you pick two words that argue with each other?'

Phase 4: compressed conflict

The teacher asks for compressed conflict as outgrowth of the personal analogy: 'Can you pick two words that argue with each other?'

Student: '*Used* and *clean*'.

Student: '*Duty* and *what you want to do*.'

Teacher: 'How can we put that more poetically?'

Student: '*Duty* versus *inclination*.'

Student: '*Duty* versus *whim*.'

Student: '*Discouraging fun*.'

Student: '*Angry game*.'

Teacher: 'All right. What one do you like best? Which one has the truest ring of conflict?' Teacher ends the enumeration of possible compressed conflicts and asks them to select one. The teacher furnishes the criterion: 'Which has the truest ring of conflict?'

Class: '*Angry game*.'

Teacher: 'All right. Can you think of a direct analogy, an example from the animal world, of *angry game*?'

Phase 5: direct analogy

Recycling the analogies, compressed conflict is not explored but serves as the basis of the next direct analogy, an example from the animal world of 'angry game'. There is no mention of the original.

Student: 'A lion in the cage at the circus.'
Student: 'Rattlesnake.'
Student: 'A pig ready for slaughter.'
Student: 'A bear when it's attacking.'
Student: 'Bullfrog.'
Student: 'A bird protecting its young.'
Student: 'Bullfight.'
Student: 'A fish being caught.'
Student: 'A skunk.'
Student: 'A horse.'
Student: 'A charging elephant.'
Student: 'A fox hunt on horseback.'
Student: 'Rodeo.'
Student: 'Porcupine.'
Teacher: 'Does anyone know where we are?'
Student: 'We're trying to put personality into Eric, trying to make him more original.'
Teacher: 'All right. Which of all the things you just thought of do you think would make the most exciting direct analogy?' (The class chooses the bullfight.) The teacher ends the enumeration of direct analogies. Again, he has the students select one but he gives the criterion: 'Which of all the things you just thought of do you think would make the most *exciting* direct analogy?'
Teacher: 'Now we go back to Eric. How can we get the bullfight to describe Eric for us? Does anyone know what I mean by that?'
The class doesn't respond. The students are not into the analogy of the bullfight yet.
Teacher: 'All right. What do we know about a bullfight?' The teacher gets students to explore the characteristics of the bullfight, the analogy.
Student: 'He'll have to be the bull or the matador. I say he's the bull.'
Student: 'Bull runs into the ring and he's surrounded by strangeness.'
Student: 'They stick things into him and goad him . . .'
Student: '. . . from horses and from the ground.'
Student: 'But sometimes he doesn't get killed.'
Student: 'And every time the bull is downgraded the crowd yells.'
Teacher: 'What happens at the end?' The teacher tries to obtain more information about the analogy.
Student: 'They drag him off with horses.'
Student: 'How do they finish him off?'
Student: 'A short sword.'
Teacher: 'How can we use this information to tell us something about Eric? How will you talk about Eric in terms of the material we've developed about a bullfight?'

Phase 6: re-examination of the original task

This phase consists of getting students to make comparisons and returning to the original problem or task.

Student: 'He's the bull.'

Student: 'He's the matador.'

Student: 'If he's the bull, then the matador is society.'

Teacher: 'Why don't you write something about Eric in terms of the bullfight? Talk about his personality and the outward signs of it. The reader opens your story about Eric and he reads. It is your reader's first introduction to Eric.' There is a pause while the students write.

Teacher: 'All finished? All right, let's read your stuff, from left to right.' Here are a few examples of the students' writing:

In rage, running against a red neon flag and blinded by its shadow, Eric threw himself down on the ground. As if they were going to fall off, blood throbbed in his ears. No use fighting any more. The knife wound in his side; the metallic jeers that hurt worse than the knife; the flash of uniforms and the flushed faces of the crowd made him want to vomit all over their clean robes.

He stood there in the middle of the street staring defiantly at the crowd. Faces leered back at him. Scornful eyes, huge red mouths, twisted laughs; Eric looked back as the crowd approached and drew his hand up sharply as one man began to speak. 'Pipe down kid. We don't want any of your nonsense.'

He was enclosed in a ring. People cheering all around for his enemy. He has been trained all his life to go out and take what he wanted and now there was an obstacle in his course. Society was bearing down and telling him he was all wrong. He must go to them and he was becoming confused. People should cheer at the matador.

The matador hunts his prey. His claim to glory is raised by the approaching approval of the crowd. For although they brought all their holiday finery, the bull is goaded, and the matador smiles complacently. You are but my instrument and I hold the sword.

(Gordon 1970: 7–11)

The synectics model has stimulated students to see and feel the original idea (a gangster or hood, described in stereotypic terms) in a variety of fresh ways. If they had been solving a problem, we would expect that they would see it more richly and increase the solutions they could explore.

USING SYNECTICS IN THE CURRICULUM

Synectics is designed to increase the creativity of both individuals and groups. Sharing the synectics experience can build a feeling of community among students. Students learn about their fellow classmates as they watch them react to an idea or problem. Thoughts are valued for their potential contribution to the group process, while synectics procedures help create a community of equals in which simply having a thought is the sole basis for status. This norm and that of playfulness quickly give support to even the most timid participant.

Synectics procedures may be used with students in all areas of the curriculum, the sciences as well as the arts. They can be applied to both teacher-student discussion in the classroom and to teacher-made materials for the students. The products or vehicles of synectics activity need not always be written: they can be oral, or they can take the form of role plays, paintings and graphics, or simply changes in behaviour.

We have found that synectics can be used with all ages, though with very young children it is best to stick to imagination-stretching exercises. Beyond this, adjustments are the same as for any other approach to teaching – take care to work within their experience, make rich use of concrete materials, pay atttention to pacing and explicit outlining of procedures.

The model often works effectively with students who withdraw from more 'academic' learning activities because they are not willing to risk being wrong. Conversely, high achieving students who are only comfortable giving a response they are sure is 'right' often feel reluctant to participate. We believe that for these reasons alone, synectics is valuable to everyone.

Synectics combines easily with other models. It can stretch concepts being explored with the information processing family; it can open up dimensions of social issues explored through role playing, group investigation or jurisprudential thinking; and it can expand the richness of problems and feelings opened up by other models in the personal family of models.

The following transcript illustrates the use of synectics to enlarge upon an academic concept. It was preceded by two concept attainment lessons, one on the concept of oxymorons and one on the concept of small, wealthy countries. Thus although this was the students' first experience with synectics, they understood the characteristics of oxymorons and were able to construct them in Phase 4 of the lesson.

Phase I: description of present condition

The teacher asks students to write a brief characterization of the world's small, wealthy countries. The students have just finished analysing a statistical data set on these countries.

Phase 2: direct analogies (and examples of student responses)

How is the Panama Canal like a bathtub? (drains)
How is the Panama Canal like a videotape? (long, encased, continuous, viewed)
How is a videotape like a book? (information, pictures)
How is viewing a videotape like dancing? (action, movement)
How is a dream like a skateboard? (falling, adventurous, exhilarating)
How is a skateboard like a blender? (spinning, wipe-out)

Phase 3: personal analogies (and examples of student responses)

Be the Panama Canal. It's midnight and a long string of ships has just begun their passage from the Pacific to the Atlantic. How do you feel? (wet, sleepy)

A huge ship, just barely able to clear both sides of the locks, enters the first lock. How do you feel? (nervous, stop!)

Pilots are getting on and off of ships. How do you feel about the pilots? (friends, protectors)

The tide is coming in with the ships from the Pacific. How do you feel about the tides? (smelly, regular, necessary)

Be a raincloud. You're moving into a clear, blue sky. Inside you are hundreds of little people with buckets. How do you feel about these little people? (laughter, 'go for it')

You move nearer a town. What are you thinking? (gotcha!)

At a signal from you, all the little people begin emptying their buckets. How do you feel? (relieved, light)

You're almost empty. You're starting to break up and you see a little wisp of yourself disappearing on the breeze. How do you feel? (nostalgic, sad)

Phase 4: compressed conflicts (and actual student responses)

lonely friendship
accustomed newness
apprehensive relief
encased adventure
archaically new
friendly enemy
descending escalation
fictional facts

Phase 5: direct analogies (and actual student responses)

What's an example of a 'lonely friendship'? (trying to resume a friendship after an argument or fight)

What is a 'fictional fact'? (a fantasy, like *Alice in Wonderland*)

Phase 6: re-examination of the original task (and actual student responses)

Think of our small, wealthy countries in terms of 'apprehensive relief'. (In the case of Kuwait, Hussein is out but it could happen again; Hong Kong is prosperous but worried about China and 1997; Qatar could be swallowed up, they're so small they need a bodyguard; their wealth is based on oil, which could run out or the world market could change with new kinds of fuels; etc.)

The use of synectics following analysis of data on the world's small, wealthy countries enabled students to elaborate their understanding of these countries. Initial data analysis left the students with an impression that these countries have no problems (with the exception of Kuwait). The synectics process moved students toward a more differentiated view of the countries which enabled them to hypothesize weaknesses as well as strengths in their relative world positions.

Another use of synectics is the development of alternative points of view toward social issues, the 'breaking of set' when considering solutions. The lesson described below occurred in India with a group of secondary students who were asked to consider the issue of career women in their modern culture. Often this topic does not even come up for discussion because the traditional cultural prescriptions for male and female roles are so powerful. Ironically, because access to higher education is based solely on merit, women comprise about half the college and university populations of India, although few women attempt to pursue a career after marriage. Since virtually all Indian women marry, an enormous human resource is being lost to a nation which sorely needs it.

(Note: this lesson was conducted in English, a second language for all the students in the session. Their native tongues were either Hindi or Marathi.)

TEACHER'S LESSON PLAN

Phase 1: description of present condition

Write a paragraph about career women in India.

Phase 2: direct analogies (and sample student responses)

How is a feather like a butterfly? (attractive, soft, flight, pursued)
How are scissors like a cactus? (sharp, sting)
How is a snake like a pillow? (slippery, gives you nightmares)
How is ping-pong like getting married? (risk, battle, ups and downs)

Phase 3: personal analogies (and sample student responses)

Be a tiger. Good morning, tigers, how do you feel? (grand, kingly, hungry, majestic, untrustworthy)

As you walk through the forest, you come upon a large body of water. You look out over the water and see a whale. What are you thinking, tigers? (greedy, breakfast, threatened, dumbstruck)

Be a feather. Tell me about yourselves, feathers. (no worries, fragile, independent, tramp)

Phase 4: compressed conflicts

Using words you've generated, construct word pairs that seem to fight each other, word pairs that have a lot of tension or incongruity:

beautiful nightmare
carefully threatened
attractive tramp
dangerously attractive
majestically greedy
grandly majestic

Now select one or two word pairs that have a great deal of incongruity:

beautiful nightmare
dangerously attractive

Phase 5: direct analogies

What is an example of a beautiful nightmare? What is dangerously attractive?

Phase 6: re-examination of the original task

Write another paragraph on career women, using the point of view of one of our oxymorons. You don't have to use the actual words of the compressed conflicts, but try to capture the meaning of the word pairs.

Here are some of the results, comparing the original (*before*) writing with those produced at the end of the exercise (*after*):

Before. If the career woman is married, then the couple gets along with each other only if the husband too pursues an equally good career. Otherwise they tend to split up as the men try to dominate the women, but the women don't like it so they must pursue a career only if it does not interfere with the bringing up of the children.

After. A career woman can succeed if she is dangerously attractive, especially if she is in the science department. People tend to feast their eyes with her in their sight and leave their stubbornness behind. Then the customer or client realizes later that he has had a beautiful nightmare if the material or the product from the dangerously attractive woman proves to be unworthy of being bought.

Before. Usually a woman should decide before taking up a career because especially in India if a woman decides to take up a career she's obstructed by her family. I think you can't look after your own family and a career together and usually men do not want their wives to have a career.

After. A career woman can be equally dangerous and attractive. She can be dangerous to people in the sense that she threatens them and when she gets a task accomplished she can be equally sweet or attractive to them.

Before. What do men feel about career women? They generally think, rather chauvinistically, that women are stupid, inefficient, miserable, subordinate co-workers. So, it is natural for men to feel that when they come face to face with career women they have been brought down to earth. An inferiority complex is expressed, giving vent to anger, jealousy, envy and irritation. But it takes time to realize that career women are generally much more determined and ambitious to make large strides in a severely male-dominated world and once this is realized I think men and women can really work together in one efficient team.

After. A career woman does give most men beautiful nightmares, some because they have to work in close contact with her and some because they do not want to have a female boss. A career woman has, in my opinion, an inbuilt tendency to be charmingly attractive and complimentary when presented with well-done tasks and dangerous when work is performed inefficiently and haphazardly.

Participation in a synectics group invariably creates a unique shared experience that fosters interpersonal understanding and a sense of community. Members learn about one another as each person reacts to the common event in his or her unique way. Individuals become acutely aware of their dependence on the various perceptions of other group members. Each thought, no matter how prosaic, is valued for its potential catalytic effect on one's own thoughts.

RESEARCH

Educators and researchers other than Gordon have explored the use and effectiveness of learning to think metaphorically. Judith and Donald Sanders' (1984) work is particularly useful for the range of explicit applications for stimulating creativity through metaphoric activity. We have found this source to be particularly useful with teachers, for we have noticed that many educators are not automatically aware of the spectrum of useful applications for models designed to induce divergent thinking.

For some reason, many of us think of 'creativity' as an aptitude that defines talent in the arts, especially writing, painting and sculpture. The creators of these models, however, believe that this 'creative aptitude' can be improved; it has applications in nearly every human endeavour and, thus, in every curriculum area. By providing illustrations in the setting of goals, the development of empathy, the study of values, a variety of areas of problem solving and the increase of perspectives for viewing topics, the Sanders make a clear and convincing case for the power of these models in expanding student thinking.

Newby and Ertner (1994) have conducted a nice series of studies where they taught students to use analogies to approach the learning of advanced physiological concepts by college students. Their results confirm the experience we have had with teaching synectics to primary and secondary students: the analogies both enhanced immediate and long-term learning and increased the pleasure the students had in learning the material. Similarly Glynn's (1994) study in science teaching indicates that using analogies in textual material enhances both short- and long-term learning. The inquiry into more efficient and powerful learning and teaching continues!

REFLECTIONS

The most effective use of synectics develops over time. It has short-term results in stretching views of concepts and problems, but when students are exposed to it repeatedly they can learn how to use it with increasing skill – and they learn to enter a metaphoric mode with increasing ease and completeness. In Hempshill Hall school, for example, pupils were well used to 'metaphoric thinking'. They coped easily with the dissonance inherent in the synectics models. This was because most teachers were so familiar with the structure of the model that they integrated it almost intuitively into their lesson plans.

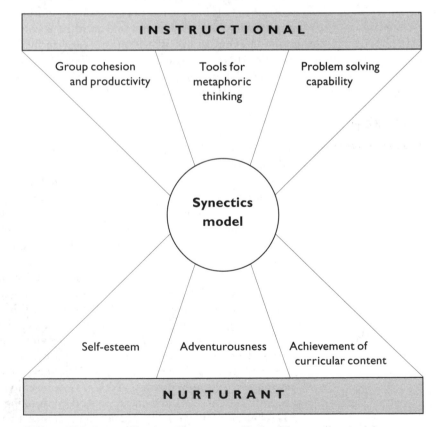

Figure 5.1 Instructional and nurturant effects of the synetics model

The synectics model contains strong elements of both instructional and nurturant values. Because he believed that the creative process could be developed, specially through direct training, Gordon designed synectics for 'creativity training' of individuals and groups. Synectics is applied, however, not only to develop general creative power but also to develop creative responses over a variety of subject matter domains. To this end, teachers using synectics emphasize a social environment that encourages creativity; they use group cohesion to generate energy that enables the participants to function interdependently in a metaphoric world. Figure 5.1 displays the instructional and nurturant effects of the synectics model of teaching and learning; Table 5.1 shows the syntax of a model of learning that helps students create something new.

Table 5.1 Syntax of the synectics model of learning and teaching

Phase 1: description of present condition
The teacher has students describe the situation or the situation as they see it now.

Phase 2: direct analogy
Students suggest direct analogies, select one and explore (describe) it further.

Phase 3: personal analogy
Students 'become' the analogy they selected in phase 2.

Phase 4: compressed conflict
Students take their descriptions from phases 2 and 3, suggest several compressed conflicts and choose one.

Phase 5: direct analogy
Students generate and select another direct analogy, based on the compressed conflict.

Phase 6: re-examination of the original task
The teacher has students move back to the original task or problem and use the last analogy and/or the entire synectics experience.

6 Learning mnemonically

The only way people come to appreciate the real power of the link-word method is to learn to use it themselves to learn new stuff – the more abstract and unfamiliar the better. Folks can't just put it forward as something that is 'good for the kids'. You have to feel it to be able to teach it well. Come to think of it, maybe that's true of all the models.

Mike McKibbin to Bruce Joyce, August 1980

Our final example from the information processing family is mnemonics. As a model of learning, mnemonics assists students to master large amounts of information and to gain conscious control of their learning processes, as the following examples illustrate.

SCENARIO I

The Phoenix High School social studies department has developed a set of mnemonics that are combined with inductive activities to teach the students the names and locations of the Planet Earth's 177 countries, plus basic demographic knowledge about each of them – population, *per capita* GNP, type of government and life expectancy. The students work in groups using mnemonics like the following one, which is designed to teach the names and locations of the Central American countries.

The exercise begins with the blank map of Central America with the countries numbered. The leader describes an imaginary tour they are about to take: 'Imagine that we're about to take a tour of Central America. Our group has learned that there has been a great deal of Spanish influence on the language and the dissemination of a religion based on the Christian Saviour – thus, we will see many signs in Spanish and will see mission churches with their distinctive bell towers. We know that the Spanish came for riches and that they expected to find a *rich coast*. We also know we will have to be careful about the water and we will carry a lot of *nickels* that we will use to buy bottled water. We are going to drive little Hondas, rather than taking a bus, and we will wear Panama hats for identifying our tour group members.'

Then the leader points to the first country, Panama, shows a first cartoon and says, 'The link word for Panama is *Panama hat*.' The group repeats the link word. The leader then points to the second country and shows a second cartoon, saying 'This country stands for the rich coast the Spanish were looking for, which is Costa Rica. The link word for Costa Rica is *rich coast*.' The group repeats the link word and the names of the countries as the leader points to them: 'Panama, Panama hat, Costa Rica, rich coast.' The exercise continues. 'The link word for Nicaragua is *nickel water* or *nickel agua*, and El Salvador is *Saviour*.' The group repeats the names of the countries and the link words in order as the leader points to the country and shows a relevant cartoon.

The leader proceeds to introduce the link word for Honduras by saying, 'We get bored a little and decide to have a *Honda Race* in our little cars.' He proceeds to Guatemala by pointing out that it has the largest population in Central America and that the link word is *gotta lotta*. Finally, pointing to the seventh country, he reminds them about the bell towers and that the sound from them is *belleeeezzz*. The group then names the countries and the link words as the leader points to them in turn.

Over the next couple of days the group members study the map, the names of the countries and the link words until they know them backward and forward. They also consult a database containing information on population, birth and death rates, *per capita* income, health care and such, and classify the countries seeking correlations among those variables. (Are level of education and life expectancy correlated? and so forth.)

In this way they proceed to examine the regions of the world, comparing and contrasting the countries and learning the names and locations of enough of them that the atlas will seem a familiar place. Eventually, of course, the study goes beyond names, locations and demographics and proceeds to rich information about a sample of the countries.

SCENARIO 2

John Pennoyer is bilingual coordinator of Las Pulgas school district. He works with the teachers to ensure that all the students learn Spanish and English simultaneously. Half of the students come to school with English as their primary language; the other half speak Spanish. The students work together to generate link words and pronunciation guides for the two languages.

One of the fifth grade classes has generated the following list as part of an introduction to Spanish for several students who have newly transferred to their school.

Spanish words

por favor (poor faBORE)	please [for favour]
gracias (GRA see ahs)	thank you [grace to you]
está bién (essTA bee en)	all right; ok [it's be good]
adiós (ahDYOHS)	goodbye
buenos días (BWEnos DEEahs)	good morning [bonnie day]

buenas tardes (BWEnas TARdays)	good afternoon [bonnie late day]
buenas noches (BWEnas NOchays)	good evening [bonnie night]
hasta mañana (AHstah manYAHna)	until tomorrow [no haste, man]

The phonetic pronunciation guides are in parentheses, followed by English equivalents. The link words are in square brackets and are designed to provide the flavour of the sounds in English, and a sense of the meanings. The new students study the words, associating the new (to them) Spanish words with the English equivalents and the link words.

SCENARIO 3

Imagine a group of students who are presented with the task of learning the names of the presidents of the United States and the order in which they served. Previously, the students have learned to count from 1 to 40 mnemonically. That is, each number is represented by a rhyming word that has an image attached to it. *One* is *bun*, *two* is *shoe*, and so on. Also each set of number decades (1 to 10, 11 to 20) is connected to a location or setting. The decade 1 to 10 is represented by a spring garden scene, 11 to 20 by a summer beach scene, 21 to 30 by an autumn football scene, and 31 to 40 by a winter snow scene.

Now, capitalizing on this system of number associations, the name and order of each president is presented to the students in terms of the scene, the mnemonic for the number, and a word, called a *link word*, associated with the president's name. Thus Lincoln (link), number 16 (sticks), is presented with an illustration of a sandcastle on a beach encircled by a set of sticks which are linked together. Similar illustrations are used for the other presidents. The students study the pictures and the words. They are given a test right after they study and again 60 days later.

How effective was this experience? Did the students learn more than other students who tried to memorize the names and their order using the usual procedures for the same length of time? The answer is yes. In this and other studies, students are being taught unfamiliar material much more quickly than usual through the application of various mnemonic devices (Pressley *et al.* 1982: 83).

MNEMONICS AS A MODEL OF LEARNING AND TEACHING

The humble task of memorizing is with us throughout our lives. From the moment of birth, a world of new artefacts and events is presented to us and has to be sorted out. Moreover, many of the elements of our world have been named by those who have come before us. We have to learn large quantities of words, and we have to learn to connect them to the objects, events, actions and qualities that they represent. In other words, we have to learn a meaningful language.

In any new area of study, a major task is learning the important words and definitions – the languages, if you will – that pertain to the area. To deal with chemistry we have to learn the names of the elements and their structural properties. To study a continent we have to learn the names of its countries, its major geographical features, the important events in its human history and so on. Initial foreign language learning involves developing a vocabulary of words that look and sound unfamiliar.

The study of memory has a long history. Although 'the goal of a unified coherent and generally satisfying theory of human memory' (Estes 1976: 11) has not yet been achieved, progress has been made. A number of teaching principles are being developed whose goals are both to teach memorization strategies and to help students study more effectively.

For instance, the material on which a particular teacher chooses to focus will affect what information the students retain. 'Many items are presented to an individual in a short time, and only those to which attention is directed enter into memory, and only those receiving rehearsal are maintained long enough to secure the processing necessary to establish a basis for long-term recall' (Estes 1976: 7). In other words, if we do not pay attention to something, we are not likely to remember it. Second, we need to attend to it in such a way that we are rehearsing later recall of it. For example, as we wander through a forest, if we do not look carefully at the tree trunks, we are unlikely to remember them, although some visual images may be retained in a haphazard fashion. Second, even if we notice them, we need to use the information, for example by comparing different trees, in order to remember it. When we rehearse, we develop *retrieval cues*, which are the basis for sorting through our memories at later times and locating information.

Short-term memories are often associated with sensory experiences of various kinds. When we are exposed to the wine called Chablis, we may remember it as straw-coloured and tasting a certain way. For long-term recall we may associate things according to *episodic* cues – that is, having to do with the sequences of experience to which we have been exposed. In English history, for example, we may remember Edward VII as the king who followed Queen Victoria. They are connected in time, and their episodes in history are connected to one another. *Categorial* cues, on the other hand, involve conceptualizations of the material. When we compare communities, for example, we form concepts that provide a basis for describing those communities in relation to one another. In other words, we replace specific items with categories and this categorization provides us with the basis for memory.

Both scholarly and popular sources agree that the ability to remember is fundamental to intellectual effectiveness. Far from being a passive, trivial activity, memorizing and remembering are active pursuits. The capacity to take information, to integrate it meaningfully and later to retrieve it at will is the product of successful memory learning. Most important, individuals can improve this capacity to memorize material so that they can recall it later. That is the objective of this model.

ONE MNEMONIC MODEL: THE LINK-WORD METHOD

Over the last ten years an important line of research has been conducted on what is termed the *link-word method*. The result is a considerable advance in knowledge about memorization as well as the development of a system that has practical implications for the design of instructional materials, for classroom teaching and tutoring, and for students.

The method has two components, assuming that the learning task is to master unfamiliar material. The first component provides the students with familiar material to link with the unfamiliar items. The second provides an association to establish the meaning of the new material. For example, when the task involves new foreign language words, one link ties the sounds to those of words in English. The second ties the new word to a representation of its meaning. For example, the Spanish word *carta* (postal letter) might be linked to the English word *cart* and a picture showing a letter inside a shopping cart (Pressley *et al.* 1982: 62).

Teaching the link-word model

For the teacher, the major labour is in preparation. Generating the links, and in some cases creating visual materials or working with students to create them, are the chief activities involved. Once the presentations have been prepared, the delivery is rather straightforward. Let us look at an example from the United States.

This exercise is similar to the one described in Scenario 2 at the beginning of the chapter and is part of a global literacy programme. The link words are phonetic and are created in a sequence following a made-up story of a career woman in the United States; all have accompanying cartoons. We begin with the map of the Middle East with seven of the countries numbered in the order in which they will be memorized.

Our career woman is recounting the beginning of her day. 'I got up', she says, and '*I ran* downstairs.' The *I ran* and its cartoon are the links to Iran. Then she says, 'I took the dishes from the *rack*.' *Rack*, with its cartoon, are links to Iraq. She continues, 'I fixed the children bowls of *Serios*.' *Serios*, with the cartoon, are links to Syria. 'I fixed myself some English muffins and took out the *jar of jam*.' *Jar of jam*, with its cartoon, are the links to Jordan. 'I also fixed myself a cup of tea and sliced a *lemon* for it.' *Lemon* is the link, with its cartoon, for Lebanon. 'Finally, I ran for the *rail*road train.' *Rail*road, with its cartoon, is the link for Israel. 'When I got to my office, I was so hot and thirsty I ran straight to the vending machine and got a *soda* to pick me up.' *Soda* (*sody*) is the link for Saudi Arabia.

These are phonetic links, which, with the illustrations, help the students connect the words (new to them) with known words and phrases and visualizations to help anchor the new material in association with familiar words, pictures and actions. The somewhat humorous and absurd tone helps make the links vivid.

Useful concepts and definitions for using this model

The following concepts are principles and techniques for enhancing our memory of learning material.

Awareness. Before we can remember anything we must give atten-tion to, or concentrate on, the things or idea to be remembered. 'Observation is essential to original awareness' (Lorayne and Lucas 1966: 6).

Association. The basic memory rule is, 'You can remember any new piece of information if it is associated to something you already know or remember' (Lorayne and Lucas 1966: 7). For example, to help students remember the spelling of *piece*, teachers will give the cue a *piece* of *pie*, which helps with both spelling and meaning.

The major limitation of cues is that they apply only to one specific thing. We can't use the phrase *a piece of pie* for more than the spelling of *piece*. In addition we usually need to remember a number of ideas. To be broadly applicable a memory system should apply more than once and should link several thoughts or items.

Link system. The heart of the memory procedure is connecting two ideas, with the second idea triggering yet another one, and so on. Although generally we only expend energy to learn meaningful material, an illustration with material that is not potentially useful helps us see how the method works. Suppose, for example, you want to remember the following five words in order: *house, glove, chair, stove, tree.* (There is no earthly reason why you would want to.) You should imagine an unusual picture, first with a house and a glove, then with a glove and a chair. For example, in the first picture you might imagine a glove opening the front door of a house, greeting a family of gloves. The second picture might be a huge glove holding a tiny chair. Taking the time to concentrate making up these images and then to visualize them will develop associations that link them in order.

Many memory problems deal with the association of two ideas. We often want to associate names and dates or places, names and ideas, words and their meaning, or a fact that establishes a relationship between two ideas.

Substitute-word system. The substitute-word system is a way of making 'an intangible, tangible and meaningful' (Lorayne and Lucas 1966: 21). It is quite simple. Merely take any word or phrase that seems abstract and 'think of something . . . that sounds like, or reminds you of, the abstract material and can be pictured in your mind' (p. 22). Remember when you used to say 'I'll ask her' in order to remember the state of Alaska. If you want to remember the name *Darwin*, you might visualize a dark wind. The concept of force can be represented by a fork. The

Cartoons 6.1 and 6.2

pictures you construct represent words, thoughts or phrases. Cartoons 6.1 and 6.2 are two examples of substitute link words and graphics that we use when introducing students to the names of the European countries.

PHASES OF THE MODEL

The model of teaching that we have developed from the work of Pressley, Levin and their associates includes four phases: attending to the material, developing connections, expanding sensory images and practising recall. These phases are based on the principle of attention and the techniques for enhancing recall.

Here is a brief description of the four phases of this model.

Phase 1 calls for activities that require the learner to concentrate on the learning material and organize it in a way that helps that learner remember it. Generally this includes focusing on what needs to be remembered – the major ideas and examples. Underlining is one way to do this. Listing the ideas separately and rephrasing them in one's own words is another task that forces attention. Finally, reflecting on the material, comparing ideas, determining the relationship among the ideas is a third attending activity.

Phase 2: once the material to be learned has been clarified and evaluated, several memory techniques should be used to develop connections with what is to be learned. Phase 2 includes using such techniques as the link words, substitute words (in the case of abstractions), and key words for long or complex passages. The notion is to connect the new material to familiar words, pictures or ideas, and to link images or words together.

Phase 3: once the initial associations have been identified, the images can be enhanced (phase 3) by asking the student to associate with more than one sense and by generating humorous dramatizations through ridiculous association and exaggeration. At this time the images can be revised for greater recall power.

In *phase 4* the student is asked to practise recall of the material.

The memory model is applicable to all curriculum areas where material needs to be memorized. It can be used with groups (a chemistry class mastering the table of elements) or individuals (a student learning a poem, story, speech, or part in a play). Although it has many uses in teacher-led 'memory sessions', it has its widest application after students have mastered it and can use it independently. Thus the model should be taught so that dependence on the teacher is decreased and students can use the procedures whenever they need to memorize. The students are taught the following steps.

1 Organizing information to be learned. The more information is organized the easier it is to learn and retain. Information can be organized by categories. The concept attainment, inductive and advance organizer models assist memory by helping students associate the material in the categories. Consider the following list of words from a popular spelling series, in the order the spelling book presents them to the children:

soft	plus	cloth	frost	song
trust	luck	club	sock	pop
cost	lot	son	won	

Suppose we ask the children to classify them by beginnings, endings and the presence of vowels. The act of classification requires the children to scrutinize the words and associate words containing similar elements. They can then name the categories in each classification (the *c* group and the *st* group), calling further attention to the common attributes of the group. They can also connect words that fit together (*pop song, soft cloth*, etc.). They can then proceed to rehearse the spellings of one category at a time. The same principle operates over other types of material – say, number facts, etc. Whether categories are provided to students or whether they create them, the purpose is the same. Also information can be selected with categories in mind. The above list is, to outward appearances, almost random. A list that deliberately and systematically provides variations would be easier to organize (it would already have at least implicit categories within it).

2 Ordering information to be learned. Information learned in series, especially if there is meaning to the series, is easier to assimilate and retain. For example, if we wish to learn the names of the states of Australia it is easier if we always start with the same one (say, the largest) and proceed in the same order. Historical events by chronology are more easily learned than events sorted randomly. Order is simply another way of organizing information. We could have the students alphabetize their list of spelling words.

3 Linking information to familiar material (sounds and meanings are both given consideration). Suppose we are learning the names of the states. We can connect *Georgia* to *George*, *Louisiana* to *Louis*, *Maryland* to *Marry* or *Merry*, and so on. Categorizing the names of the states or ordering them by size, or ordering them within region, provides more associations.

4 Linking information to visual representations. Maryland can be linked to a picture of a marriage, Oregon to a picture of a gun, Maine to a burst water main, and so forth. Letters and numerals can be linked to something that evokes both familiar sounds and images. For example, *one* can be linked to *bun* and a picture of a boy eating a bun, *b* to a bee and a picture of a bee. Those links can be used over and over again. 'April is the cruellest month, breeding lilacs out of the dead land' is easier remembered thinking of an ominous spring, bending malevolently over the spring flowers.

5 Linking information to associated information. A person's name, linked to information such as a well-known person having the same name, a soundalike, and some personal information, is easier to remember than the name rehearsed by itself. Learning the states of Australia while thinking of the points of the compass and the British origins of many of the names (New South Wales) is easier than learning them in order alone.

6 Devices that make the information vivid are also useful. Lorayne and Lucas favour 'ridiculous association', where information is linked to absurd associations. ('The silly two carries his twin two on his back so they are really four.') Others favour the use of dramatization and vivid illustrations (such as counting the basketball players on two teams to illustrate that five and five equal ten).

7 Rehearsal (practice) is always useful, and students benefit from knowledge of results. Students who have not had past success with tasks requiring memorization will benefit by having relatively short assignments and clear, timely feedback linked to their success.

RESEARCH

An important finding from the research is that people who master material more quickly and who retain it longer generally use more elaborate strategies for memorizing material. They use mnemonics – ways of helping memorization. The less effective memorizers generally use 'rote' procedures. They 'say' what is to be memorized over and over again until they believe it is implanted in their memories.

A second important finding is that devices like the link-word method are even more elaborate than the methods used by the better 'natural' memorizers – that is, they require more mental activity than do the rote procedures. When first confronted by the presidential illustrations discussed earlier, many teachers respond, 'But why add all the extra stuff? Isn't it hard enough to master the names of the presidents and their order? Why add words like *link* and *stick* and pictures of sandcastles on a summer beach?'

The answer is that the additional associations provide a richer mental context and the linking process increases the cognitive activity. The combination of activity and associations provides better 'anchors' within our information processing systems.

Does the key-word method (focusing on critical words in a paragraph) help students who are ordinarily good, poor and average memorizers? Apparently so (Pressley and Dennis-Rounds 1980). Further, it appears to help students who are below average in verbal ability, who might have been expected to have greater difficulty with complex learning strategies. In addition, as students use the method, they seem to transfer it to other learning tasks. Thus mnemonics can be taught so that students can use them independently of the teacher. The students, in other words, can develop systems for making up their own links.

Finally, even young (kindergarten and first grade) children can profit from mnemonics (Pressley *et al.* 1981a, 1981b). Obviously they have greater difficulty generating their own links, but they can benefit when links are provided to them.

The effect sizes from the research on the link-word method are impressive. Even in Atkinson's (1966) early studies, the link-word method was about 50 per cent more effective than conventional rote methods. That is, students learned half-again more material in the same time period as students not using link words. In some of the later studies it has been twice as efficient or more (Pressley 1977; Pressley *et al.* 1981a, 1981b). Just as important, retention has been made easier. That is, more is remembered longer when link words are used.

In a very interesting recent study, Levin and Levin (1990) applied the method to teach what are generally considered 'higher order' objectives – in this case, a hierarchical system for classifying plants. They compared the effectiveness of using links to familiar concepts with a traditional graphic representation, with the hierarchy presented in a chart featuring boxes connected by lines. The links not only facilitated the learning and remembering of the hierarchical scheme but also affected problem solving.

There are two obvious uses of this research. The first is to arrange instruction so as to make it as easy as possible for students to make associations and to discourage isolated rote drill. The second is to teach students to make their own links when they are studying new material.

Some of the other models can help us here. Concept attainment provides classifications that categorize exemplars on the basis of attributes; they induce students to make contrasts with the nonexemplars. Inductive teaching causes students to build associations on the basis of common characteristics. Advance organizers provide an 'intellectual scaffolding' that ties material together, and comparative organizers link the new with the old. The scientific inquiry methods provide an experiential base for terms and an intellectual structure to 'glue' material together.

REFLECTIONS

One of the most effective forms of personal power comes from competence based on knowledge; it is essential to success and a sense of well-being. Throughout our lives we need to be able to memorize skilfully. To improve this ability increases learning power, saves time and leads to a better storehouse of information (see Table 6.1 for the syntax of the model).

Mnemonics is specifically designed to increase the capacity to store and retrieve information. But as is seen in Figure 6.1, it should also nurture a sense of intellectual power – a growing consciousness of the ability to master unfamiliar material, as well as imagery skills and attention to one's environment.

Aids to memory are used extensively in Hempshill Hall school to master the large amounts of information necessary at Key Stages 1 and 2. At Hempshill Hall this has been so successful that the pupils understand the model and invent their own link words and associations.

One of the most important outcomes of the model is the students' recognition that learning is not a mysterious, innate process over which they have no control. As Ian Hunter (1964: 302) points out:

> The mastery of some simple mnemonic system may lead some people to realize, for the first time, that they can control and modify their own mental activities. And this realization may encourage them to undertake that self-critical experimentation with their own learning and remembering procedures which is such an important part of intellectual development.

Thus awareness of how to learn and how to improve learning results in a sense of mastery and control over one's future. Finally, of course, our capacity for remembering particular material is strengthened by this model – we become more effective memorizers.

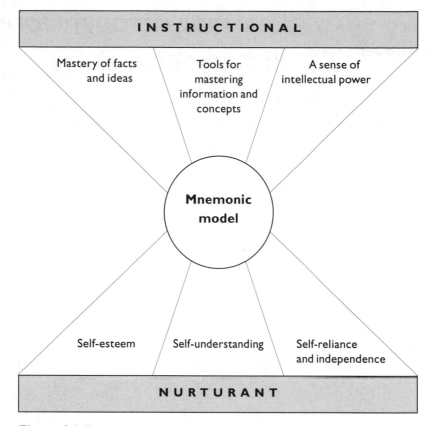

Figure 6.1 Instructional and nurturant effects of the mnemonics model

Table 6.1 Syntax of the mnemonics model of teaching and learning

---

Phase 1: attending to the material
Use techniques of underlining, listing, reflecting.

Phase 2: developing connections
Make material familiar and develop connections using key-word, substitute-
  word and link-word system techniques.

Phase 3: expanding sensory images
Use techniques of ridiculous association and exaggeration. Revise images.

Phase 4: practising recall
Practise recalling the material until it is completely learned.

---

7 Learning through cooperative disciplined inquiry

The most stunning thing about teaching people to help kids learn cooperatively is that people don't know how to do it as a consequence of their own schooling and life in this society. And, if anything is genetically driven, it's a social instinct. If it weren't for each other, we wouldn't even know who we are.

Herbert Thelen to Bruce Joyce, circa 1964

Our first example from the social family – learning from cooperative disciplined inquiry – is not a single model, but more of a continuum of learning. All the simpler forms of cooperative learning, as seen in Scenario 1, are preparations for the more rigorous, active and integrative collective action required in 'group investigation', as seen in Scenario 2. Both teachers have embarked on the task of building learning communities. They will teach the students to work together impersonally but positively, to gather and analyse information, to build and test hypotheses, and to coach one another as they develop skills. The difference in maturity between the classes will affect the degree of sophistication of their inquiry, but the basic teaching/learning process will be the same.

Each of these teachers has a variety of strategies for helping their students learn to work productively together. Each teacher is studying their students, learning how effectively they cooperate, and deciding how to design the next activities to teach them to work more effectively together.

SCENARIO 1: PARTNERS IN LEARNING

As the children enter Kelly Farmer's Year 5 classroom on the first day of the school year, they find the class list on each desk. She smiles at her pupils and says: 'Let's start by learning all our names and one of the ways we will be working together this year. You'll notice I've arranged the desks in pairs, and the persons sitting at each pair will be partners in today's activities. I want each partnership to take our class list and classify the first names by how they sound. Then we will share the groupings or categories each partnership makes. This will help us learn one another's names. It will also introduce you to one of the ways we will study spelling and several other subjects this year. I know from Mrs

Annis that you worked inductively last year so you know how to classify information, but let me know if you have any problems.' The children *do* know what to do, and within a few minutes they are ready to share their classifications:

'We put Nancy and Sally together because they end in *y*.'

'We put George and Jerry together because they sound the same at the beginning although they're spelled differently.'

'We put the three Kevins together.'

A few minutes later the pairs are murmuring together as they help one another learn to spell the list of names.

Kelly has started the year by organizing the children into a 'cooperative set', by which we mean an organization for cooperative learning. She will teach the children to work in dyads and triads which can be combined into groups of five or six. (Task- or workgroups larger than that generally have much lower productivity.) The partnerships will change for various activities. The children will learn to accept any members of the class as their partners and that they are to work with each other to try to ensure that everyone achieves the objectives of each activity.

She begins with pairs because that is the simplest social organization. In fact, much of the early training in cooperative activity will be conducted in groups of two and three because the interaction is simpler than in larger groups. She also uses fairly straightforward and familiar cognitive tasks for the initial training for the same reason – it is easier for children to learn to work together when they are not mastering complex activities at the same time. For example, she asks them to change partners, for the new partnerships to quiz each other on simple knowledge (such as of the states and their capitals) and tutor one another. She may change partnerships again and ask them to categorize sets of fractions by size. Each pupil learns how to work with any and all of the other children in a variety of tasks. Later she will teach the children to respond to the cognitive tasks of the more complex information processing models of teaching as well as more complex cooperative sets. By the end of October she expects the children to be skilful enough to be introduced to group investigation.

SCENARIO 2: GROUP INVESTIGATION – BUILDING EDUCATION THROUGH THE DEMOCRATIC PROCESS

Sue Content's Year 11 class on world geography has been studying demographic data taken from a computer program of nations of the world. Each of the nine groups of four students have analysed the data on about 20 nations and searched for correlations among the following variables: population, *per capita* GNP (gross national product), birth rate, life expectancy, education, health care services, industrial base, agricultural production, transportation systems, foreign debt, balance of payments, women's rights and natural resources.

The groups reported back what they had discovered – and what had begun as a purely academic exercise suddenly took off:

'People born in some countries have a life expectancy 20 years less than people in other countries.'

'We didn't find a relationship between levels of education and *per capita* wealth!'

'Some rich countries spend more on military facilities and personnel than some large poor ones spend on health care!'

'Women's rights don't correlate with type of government! Some democracies are less liberal than some dictatorships!'

'Some little countries are relatively wealthy because of commerce and industry. Some others just have one mineral that is valuable.'

'The United States owes other countries an awful lot of money.'

The time is ripe for group investigation. Ms Content carefully leads the students to record their reactions to the data. They make a decision to bring together the data on all the countries and find out if the groups' conclusions will apply over the entire data set. They also decide that they need to find a way of getting in-depth information about selected countries to flesh out their statistical data. But which countries? How will they test their hypotheses?

One student wonders aloud about world organizations and how they relate to the social situation of the world. They have heard of the United Nations and the European Union but are vague about how they function. One has heard about the 'Committee of Seven', but the others have not. Several have heard of NATO but are not sure how it operates. Some wonder about UNESCO, others about China and its immense population and how they fit into the global picture.

Clearly, deciding priorities for the inquiry will not be easy. However, the conditions for group investigation are present. The students are puzzled. They react differently to the various questions. They need information, and information sources are available. Ms Content smiles at her brood of young furrowed brows. 'Let's get organized. There is information we all need, and let's start with that. Then let's prioritize our questions and divide the labour to get information that will help us.'

COOPERATIVE DISCIPLINED ACTIVITY AS A MODEL OF LEARNING AND TEACHING

The assumptions that underlie the development of cooperative learning communities are straightforward:

1 The synergy generated in cooperative settings generates more motivation than do individualistic, competitive environments. Integrative social groups are, in effect, more than the sum of their parts. The feelings of connectedness produce positive energy.

2 The members of cooperative groups learn from one another. Each learner has more helping hands than in a structure that generates isolation.

3 Interacting with one another produces cognitive as well as social complexity, creating more intellectual activity that increases learning when contrasted with solitary study.

4 Cooperation increases positive feelings toward one another, reduces alienation and loneliness, builds relationships, and provides affirmative views of other people.

5 Cooperation increases self-esteem not only through increased learning but through the feeling of being respected and cared for by others in the environment.

6 Students can respond to experience in tasks requiring cooperation by increasing their capacity to work together productively. In other words, the more children are given the opportunity to work together, the better they get at it, with benefit to their general social skills.

7 Students, including primary school children, can learn from training to increase their ability to work together.

Recently interest has been renewed in research on the cooperative learning models. The more sophisticated research procedures that now exist are better able to test underlying assumptions and provide more precise estimates of their effects on academic, personal and social behaviour. Work by three groups of researchers is of particular interest (Johnson and Johnson 1974, 1981, 1993; Sharan 1980, 1990; and Slavin 1983, 1990). Using somewhat different strategies, the teams of both the Johnsons and Slavin have conducted sets of investigations that closely examine the assumptions of the social family of teaching models. Specifically, they have studied whether cooperative tasks and reward structures affect learning outcomes positively. Also they have asked whether group cohesion, cooperative behaviour and intergroup relations are improved through cooperative learning procedures. In some of their investigations they have examined the effects of cooperative task and reward structures on 'traditional' learning tasks in which students are presented with material to master.

Important for us is the question of whether cooperative groups do in fact generate the energy that results in improved learning. The evidence is largely affirmative. Classrooms where students work in pairs and larger groups, where students tutor each other and share rewards, are characterized by greater mastery of material than the common individual-study/recitation pattern. Also the shared responsibility and interaction produce more positive feelings toward tasks and others, generate better intergroup relations and result in better self-images for students with histories of poor achievement. In other words, the results generally affirm the assumptions that underlie the use of cooperative learning methods (see Sharan 1990).

Cooperative learning theorists differ in their views about whether groups should compete with one another; Slavin generally favours competition and the Johnsons cooperation. Qin et al. (1995) have recently published a complex review of research on this question and report that the cooperative structures generally generate improved learning in the important area of problem-solving.

Sharan and his colleagues (Sharan and Hertz-Lazarowitz 1980a, 1980b; Sharan and Shachar 1988) have studied group investigation; they have learned much both about how to make the dynamics of the model work and about its effects on cooperative behaviour, intergroup relations, and lower- and higher order achievement. We will discuss their research when we look at group investigation later in this chapter.

An exciting use of the cooperative procedures is in combination with models from other families, in an effort to combine the effects of several models. For example, Baveja *et al.* (1985) conducted a study in which concept and inductive procedures were carried out in cooperative groups. The effects fulfilled the promise of the marriage of the information processing and social models, and the treatment generated gains twice those of a comparison group that received intensive individual and group tutoring over the same material. Similarly, Joyce *et al.* (1989) combined cooperative learning with several other models of teaching to obtain dramatic (30 per cent to 95 per cent) increases in promotion rates with at-risk students. There were also correspondingly large decreases in disruptive activity, an obvious reciprocal of increases in cooperative and integrative behaviour.

For those for whom cooperative learning is an innovation, an endearing feature is that it is so very easy to organize students into pairs and triads. And it gets effects immediately. The combination of social support and the increase in cognitive complexity caused by the social interaction have mild but rapid effects on the learning of content and skills. In addition, partnerships in learning provide a pleasant laboratory in which to develop social skills and empathy for others. Off-task and disruptive behaviour diminish substantially. Students feel good in cooperative settings, and positive feelings toward self and others are enhanced.

Another positive feature is that the students with poorer academic histories benefit so quickly. Partnerships increase involvement, and the concentration on cooperation has the side-effect of reducing self-absorption and increasing responsibility for personal learning. Whereas the effect sizes on academic learning are modest but consistent, the effects on social learning and personal esteem can be considerable when comparisons are made with individualistic classroom organization.

Curiously, we have found that some parents and teachers believe that students who are the most successful in individualistic environments will not profit from cooperative environments. Sometimes this belief is expressed as 'gifted students prefer to work alone'. A mass of evidence contradicts that belief (Joyce 1991; Slavin 1991). Perhaps a misunderstanding about the relationship between individual and cooperative study contributes to the persistence of the belief. Developing partnerships does not imply that individual effort is not required. In Scenario 4 at the beginning of the book, all the individuals in Mary Thomas's

Year 10 class read the poems. When classifying poems together, each individual contributed ideas and studied the ideas of others. Individuals are not submerged, but are enhanced by partnerships with others. Successful students are not inherently less cooperative. In highly individualistic environments they are sometimes taught disdain for less-successful students, to their detriment as students and people, both in school and in the future.

INCREASING THE EFFICIENCY OF PARTNERSHIPS: TRAINING FOR COOPERATION

For reasons not entirely clear to us, the initial reaction of some people to the proposition that students be organized to study together is one of concern that they will not know how to work together productively. In fact, partnerships over simple tasks are not very demanding of social skills. Most students are quite capable of cooperating when they are clear about what has been asked of them. However, developing more efficient ways of working together is clearly important, and there are some guidelines for helping students become more practised and efficient: group size, complexity and practice.

Our initial illustrations are of simple dyadic partnerships over clear cognitive tasks. The reason is that the pair or dyad is the simplest form of social organization. One way to help students learn to work cooperatively is to provide practice in the simpler settings of twos and threes. Assuming we regulate complexity through the tasks we give and the sizes of groups we form, if students are unaccustomed to cooperative work, it makes sense to give the smallest size groups simple or familiar tasks to permit them to gain the experience that will enable them to work in groups of larger sizes. However, task groups larger than six persons are clumsy and require skilled leadership which students cannot provide to one another without experience or training. Actually partnerships of two, three or four are the most commonly employed.

Practice results in increased efficiency. If we begin learning with partners and simply provide practice for a few weeks, we will find that the students become increasingly productive.

Training for efficiency

There are also methods for training the students for more efficient cooperation and 'positive interdependence' (see Kagan 1990; Johnson and Johnson 1994). Simple hand signals can be used to get the attention of busy groups. One of the common procedures is to teach the students that when the instructors raise their hands, anyone who notices is to give their attention to the instructor and raise their hand also. Other students notice and raise their hands, and soon the entire instructional group is attending. This type of procedure is constructive because it works while avoiding shouting above the hubbub of the busy partnerships; it also teaches the students to participate in the management process.

Kagan has developed several procedures for teaching students to work together for goals and to ensure that all students participate equally in the group tasks. An example is what he calls 'numbered heads'. Suppose that the students are working in partnerships of three. Each member takes a number from one to three. Simple tasks are given – 'How many metaphors can you find in this page of prose?'. All members are responsible for mastery of each task. After a suitable interval, the instructor calls out one number, for example 'Number twos'. The number two persons in all groups raise their hands. They are responsible for speaking for their groups. The instructor calls on one of them. All other persons are responsible for listening and checking the answer of the person who reports. For example, if the response is 'seven', the other students are responsible for checking that response against their own. 'How many agree? Disagree?' The procedure is designed to ensure that some individuals do not become the 'learners' and 'spokespersons' for their groups while others are carried along for the ride.

Also, for tasks for which it is appropriate, pre-tests may be given. An example might be a list of words to learn to spell. After the pre-test a number of tasks might be given to help the students study the words. Then an interval might be provided for the students to tutor one another, followed by a post-test. Each group would then calculate their gain-scores (the number correct on the post-test minus the number correct on the pre-test), giving all members a stake in everyone's learning. Also, cooperative learning aside, the procedure makes clear that it is learning as expressed in *gain* that is the purpose of the exercise. When post-tests only are used, it is not clear whether anyone has actually *learned* – students can receive high marks for a score no higher than they would have achieved in a pre-test.

Sets of training tasks can help students learn to be more effective partnerships, to increase their stake in one another, and to work assiduously for learning by all.

Training for interdependence

In addition to practice and training for more efficient cooperative behaviour, procedures for helping students become truly interdependent are available. The least complex procedures involve reflection on the group process and discussions about ways of working together most effectively. The more complex procedures involve the provision of tasks that require interdependent behaviour. For example, there are card games where success depends on 'giving up' valuable cards to another player, and communication games where success requires taking the position of another. Familiar games like Charades and Pictionary are popular because they increase cohesion and the ability to put oneself in the place of the other. There are also procedures for rotating tasks so that each person moves from subordinate to superordinate tasks and where members take turns as coordinators.

The Johnsons (1994) have demonstrated that sets of these tasks can increase interdependence, empathy and role taking ability, and that students can become quite expert at analysing group dynamics and learning to create group climates that foster mutuality and collective responsibility. The role playing model of teaching, discussed in the next chapter, is designed to help students analyse their values and to work together to develop interactive frames of reference.

DIVISION OF LABOUR: SPECIALIZATION

A variety of procedures have been developed to help students learn how to help one another by dividing labour. Essentially, tasks are presented in such a way that division of labour increases efficiency. The underlying rationale is that dividing labour increases group cohesion as the team works to learn information or skills while ensuring that all members have both responsibility for learning and an important role in the group. Imagine, for example, that a class is studying Africa and is organized into groups of four. Four countries are chosen for study. One member of each team might be designated a 'country specialist'. The country specialists from all teams would gather together and study their assigned nation and become the tutors for their original groups, responsible for summarizing information and presenting it to the other members. Or, similarly, when tasks requiring memorization are presented to the class, the group will divide responsibility for creating mnemonics for aspects of the data. Or teams could take responsibility for parts of the information to be learned.

A procedure known as 'jigsaw' (Aronson et al. 1978; Slavin 1983) has been worked out to develop formal organizations for divisions of labour. It is highly structured and appropriate as an introduction to division-of-labour processes. Whereas individualistic classroom organization allows individuals to exercise their best-developed skills, division of labour procedures require students to rotate roles, developing their skills in all areas.

COOPERATIVE OR COMPETITIVE GOAL STRUCTURES

As we have already noted, some developers organize teams to compete against one another while others emphasize cooperative goals and minimize team competition. Johnson and Johnson (1993) have analysed the research and argue that the evidence favours cooperative goal structures, while Slavin (1983) argues that competition between teams benefits learning. The fundamental question is whether students are orientated toward competing with one another or with a goal. Recently several of our colleagues have organized whole classes to work cooperatively toward a goal. For example, the science department of a high school began the year in chemistry by organizing the students to master the essential features of the table of elements. In teams, they built mnemonics that were used by all the students. Within two weeks all students knew the table backward and forward, and that information served as the structural organizer for the entire course.

In a group of fifth grade classes the exploration of social studies began with memorization of the states, large cities, river and mountain systems, and other basic information about the geography of the United States. Class scores were computed (for example, 50 states times 30 students is 1,500 items). The goal was for the class as a whole to achieve a perfect score. The classes reached scores over 1,450 within a week, leaving individuals with very few items to master to reach a perfect score for the class.

Motivation: from extrinsic to intrinsic?

The issue about how much to emphasize cooperative or individualistic goal structures relates to conceptions of motivation. Sharan (1990) has argued that cooperative learning increases learning partly because it causes motivational orientation to move from the external to the internal. In other words, when students cooperate over learning tasks they become more interested in learning for its own sake rather than for external rewards. Thus students engage in learning for intrinsic satisfaction and become less dependent on praise from teachers or other authorities. The internal motivation is more powerful than the external, resulting in increased learning rates and retention of information and skills.

The frame of reference of the cooperative learning community is a direct challenge to the principles which many schools have used to guide their use of tests and rewards to students for achievement. Unquestionably one of the fundamental purposes of general education is to increase internal motivation to learn and to encourage students to generate learning for the sheer satisfaction in growing. If cooperative learning procedures (among others) succeed partly because they contribute to this goal, then the testing and reward structures that prevail in most school environments may actually retard learning. As we turn to group investigation – a powerful model that radically changes the learning environment – let us consider how different are the tasks, cooperative structures and principles of motivation we observe in many contemporary schools.

GROUP INVESTIGATION: BUILDING EDUCATION THROUGH THE DEMOCRATIC PROCESS

John Dewey's ideas have given rise to the broad and powerful model of teaching, known as group investigation, that extends the notions of cooperative learning that we have just described. As seen in Scenario 2, students are organized into democratic problem solving groups who tackle academic problems and are taught democratic procedures and scientific methods of inquiry as they proceed. The movement to practise democracy in the classroom constituted the first major reform effort in American education and generated a great deal of critical reaction. Schools' experiments with democratic-process education were subjected to serious criticism during the 1930s and 1940s; the first items of research produced by the reformers were actually developed defensively in response to questions raised by concerned citizens about whether such a degree of reliance on social purposes would retard the students' academic development.

These studies generally indicated that social and academic goals were not incompatible. The students from those schools were not disadvantaged; in many respects, in fact, they outperformed students from competitive environments where social education was not emphasized (Chamberlin and Chamberlin 1943). The hostile reaction continued, however – a seeming anomaly in a democracy whose political and commercial institutions depend so much on integrative organizational behaviour.

Educational models derived from a conception of society usually envision what human beings would be like in a very good – even utopian – society. Their educational methods aim to develop ideal citizens who could live in and enhance that society, who could fulfil themselves in and through it, and who would even be able to help create and revise it. We have had such models from the time of the Greeks. Plato's *Republic* is a blueprint for an ideal society and the educational programme to support it. Aristotle also dealt with the ideal education and society. Since their time, many other utopians have produced educational models, including St Augustine *The City of God*, Sir Thomas More *Utopia*, Comenius *The Great Didactic*, and John Locke *Some Thoughts Concerning Education*.

It was natural that attempts would be made to use teaching methods to improve society. In the United States, extensive efforts have been made to develop classroom instruction as a model of democratic process; in fact, variations on democratic process are probably more common than any other general teaching method as far as the educational literature is concerned. In terms of instructional models, *democratic process* has referred to organizing classroom groups to do any or all of the following tasks:

1 develop a social system based on and created by democratic procedures;
2 conduct scientific inquiry into the nature of social life and processes. In this case the term *democratic procedures* is synonymous with the scientific method and inquiry;
3 engage in solving a social or interpersonal problem;
4 provide an experience-based learning situation.

Given the positive effects on student learning in all domains, it is a serious mistake not to make group investigation a staple in the repertoire of all schools.

Using group investigation in the school and classroom

Herbert Thelen's group investigation model of teaching resembles the methods Dewey recommends. Group investigation attempts to combine in one teaching strategy the form and dynamics of the democratic process with the process of academic inquiry. The three concepts of inquiry, knowledge and group dynamics are central to Thelen's strategy.

Inquiry is stimulated by confrontation with a problem, and knowledge results from the inquiry. The social process enhances inquiry and is itself studied and improved. The heart of group investigation lies in its formulation of inquiry. According to Thelen (1960: 85), the concern of inquiry is 'to initiate and supervise the processes of giving attention to something; of interacting with and being stimulated by other people, whether in person or through their writing; and of reflection and re-organization of concepts and attitudes as shown in arriving at conclusions, identifying new investigations to be undertaken, taking action and turning out a better product.'

The first element of inquiry is an event the individual can react to and puzzle over – a problem to be solved. In the classroom the teacher can select content and cast it in terms of problem situations, for example 'How did our community come to be the way it is?' Simply providing a problem, however, will not generate the puzzlement that is a major energy source for inquiry. The students must add an awareness of self and a desire for personal meaning. In addition, they must assume the dual roles of participant and observer, simultaneously inquiring into the problem and observing themselves as inquirers. Because inquiry is basically a social process, students are aided in the self-observer role by interacting with, and by observing the reactions of, other puzzled people. The conflicting viewpoints that emerge also energize the students' interest in the problem.

Although the teacher can provide a problem situation, it is up to the students as inquirers to identify and formulate the problem and pursue its solution. Inquiry calls for first-hand activity in a real situation and ongoing experience that continually generates new data. The students must thus be conscious of method so that they may collect data, associate and classify ideas recalling past experience, formulate and test hypotheses, study consequences and modify plans. Finally, they must develop the capacity for reflection, the ability to synthesize overt participative behaviour with symbolic verbal behaviour. The students are asked to give conscious attention to the experience – to formulate explicitly the conclusions of the study and to integrate them with existing ideas. In this way thoughts are reorganized into new and more powerful patterns.

The development of *knowledge* is the goal of inquiry, but Thelen uses knowledge in a special way: as the application of the universals and principles drawn from past experience on to present experience. In any group learning experience, the process of discovering knowledge should be on centre stage at all times; the principles of inquiry are what counts. As Thelen (1960: 51) said:

> Knowledge is unborn experience; it is the universals incorporated into the nervous system; it is a predisposition to approach the world with inquiry; it is meaningful past experience living within itself; it is the seed of potential internal reorganization through which one keeps in touch with the changing world. Knowledge lies in the basic alternative orientations and the proposition through which new orientations can be built.

In other words, we 'try on' various ways of looking at experience, continually reinterpreting experience into workable principles and concepts.

Group dynamics – why should inquiry take place in groups? In addition to the application of scientific method, inquiry has emotional aspects – emotions rising from involvement and growing self-awareness, the seeking of personal meaning and the affect that accompanies conscious reflective behaviour. Thus Thelen (1954: 45) views a learning situation as 'one which involves the emotions of the learner'. The group is both an arena for personal needs (individuals with their anxieties, doubts and private desires) and also an instrument for solving social problems. As conflicting views impinge on individuals, they find themselves inescapably involved in the social and academic dimensions of inquiry. The individual 'is driven by very profound and very pervasive psyche needs for the kind of classroom in which he can survive as a person and find a place for himself in the organization. Algebra may mean less than nothing initially, but self-esteem, freedom of sorts, feelings of growing adequacy and stimulation that provoke him into rewarding activity are important' (p. 147). The social aspects of group investigation provide a route, therefore, to disciplined academic inquiry.

As a group confronts a puzzling situation, the reactions of individuals vary widely, and the assumptive worlds that give rise to these varied reactions are even more different than the reactions themselves. The need to reconcile this difference generates a basic challenge. The newly perceived alternatives extend the student's experience by serving both as a source of self-awareness and as a stimulant to his or her curiosity. Engaged in inquiry with a group, individuals become aware of different points of view that help them find out who they are by seeing themselves projected against the views of others. It also stimulates them: they want to know *why* differences exist and how they affect them.

PHASES OF THE MODEL

Group investigation begins by confronting the students with a stimulating problem. The confrontation may be presented verbally, or it may be an actual experience; it may arise naturally, or it may be provided by a teacher. If the students react, the teacher draws their attention to the differences in their reactions – what stances they take, what they perceive, how they organize things and what they feel. As the students become interested in their differences in reaction, the teacher draws them toward formulating and structuring the problem for themselves. Next, students analyse the required roles, organize themselves, act and report their results. Finally the group evaluates its solution in terms of its original purposes. The cycle repeats itself, either with another confrontation or with a new problem growing out of the investigation itself.

The teacher's role in group investigation is one of counsellor, consultant and friendly critic. He or she must guide and reflect the group experience over three levels: the problem solving or task level (What is the nature of the problem? What are the factors involved?); the group management level (What information do we need now? How can we organize ourselves to get it?); and the level of individual meaning (How do you feel about these conclusions? What would you do differently as a result of knowing about . . .?) (Thelen 1954: 52–3). This teaching role is a very difficult and sensitive one, because the essence of inquiry is student activity – problems cannot be imposed. At the same time, the teacher must:

- facilitate the group process,
- intervene in the group to channel its energy into potentially educative activities, and
- supervise these educative activities so that personal meaning comes from the experience (p. 13).

Intervention by the teacher should be minimal unless the group bogs down seriously.

How do students respond to the model and what does the teaching/learning interaction look like? The students react to the puzzling situation and examine the nature of their common and different reactions. They determine what kinds of information they need to approach the problem and proceed to collect relevant data. They generate hypotheses and gather the information needed to test them. They evaluate their products and continue their inquiry or begin a new line of inquiry. The central teaching moves build the cooperative social environment and teach students the skills of negotiation and conflict resolution necessary for democratic problem solving. In addition, the teacher needs to guide the students in methods of data collection and analysis, help them frame testable hypotheses, and decide what would constitute a reasonable test of a hypothesis. Because groups vary considerably in their need for structure (Hunt 1971) and their cohesiveness (Thelen 1967), the teacher cannot behave mechanically but must 'read' the students' social and academic behaviour and provide the assistance that keeps the inquiry moving without squelching it.

Group investigation requires the use of multiple sources of information. The school needs to be equipped with a first-class library that provides information and opinion through a wide variety of media; it should also be able to provide access to outside resources as well.

Children should be encouraged to investigate and to contact resource people beyond the school walls. One reason cooperative inquiry of this sort has been relatively rare is that the information and support systems were not adequate to maintain the level of inquiry; today, this should not be a problem.

Group investigation also requires flexibility from the teacher and the classroom organization. If students have not had an opportunity to experience the kind of social interaction, decision making and independent inquiry called for in this model, it may take some time before they function at a high level. On the other hand, students who have participated in classroom meetings and/or self-directed, inquiry-orientated learning will probably have an easier time. In any case, it is probably useful for the teacher to remember that the social aspects of the model may be as unfamiliar to students as the intellectual aspects and may be as demanding in terms of skill acquisition.

With young children or students new to group investigation, fairly small-scale investigations are possible; the initial confrontation can provide a narrow range of topics, issues, information and alternative activities. For example, providing an evening's entertainment for the school is more focused than resolving the energy crisis. Deciding who will care for the classroom pet, and how, is even narrower. Of course, the nature of the inquiry depends on the interests and ages of the students. Older students tend to be concerned with more complex issues. However, the skilful teacher can design inquiries appropriate to the students' abilities and to his or her own ability to manage the investigation.

In the following section we share some of the research underpinning the cooperative learning models, of which group investigation is the most complex form.

RESEARCH

As we have already noted, there have been three lines of research on ways of helping students study and learn together, one led by David and Roger Johnson, a second by Robert Slavin, and the third by Shlomo and Yael Sharan and Rachel Hertz-Lazarowitz in Israel.

Among other things, the Johnsons and their colleagues have studied the effects of cooperative task and reward structures on learning (1981, 1990, 1993). Their work on peers teaching peers has provided information about the effects of cooperative behaviour on both traditional learning tasks and the effects on values and intergroup behaviour and attitudes (1981, 1993). Their models emphasize the development of what they call 'positive interdependence', or cooperation where collective action also celebrates individual differences.

Slavin's extensive 1983 review included the study of a variety of approaches where he manipulated the complexity of the social tasks and experiments with various types of grouping. He reported success with the use of heterogeneous groups with tasks requiring coordination of group members both on academic learning and intergroup relations, and has generated a variety of strategies that employ extrinsic and intrinsic reward structures.

The Israeli team, led by Shlomo Sharan, has concentrated on group investigation, the most complex of the social models of teaching. His team has reported that the more pervasive the cooperative climate, the more positive the students are toward both the learning tasks and toward each other (Sharan and Hertz-Lazarowitz 1980a, 1980b). In addition he has hypothesized that greater social complexity would increase achievement of more complex learning goals (concepts and theories); he has both confirmed his hypothesis and found that it increased the learning of information and basic skills as well.

Some information is also available on whole-school cooperative learning. Research that compares schools has gone on for some time. In the early years, these studies were designed on a planned variation model, where schools operating from different stances toward education were compared with one another. For example, over 50 years ago the beautifully designed 'eight-year study' (Chamberlin and Chamberlin 1943) submitted the theses of the Progressive Movement (largely cooperative learning-orientated) to a serious (and generally successful) test and defended it against the suggestion that social and personal models of education were dangerous to the academic health of students. Research on unusually effective schools has found that one of their most prominent characteristics is a cooperative social climate in which all faculty and students work together to build a supportive, achievement-orientated climate. This is a strong finding from much of the recent school effectiveness and improvement research in the UK (Mortimore et al. 1988; MacGilchrist et al. 1995; Hopkins et al. 1996).

A group of secondary school teachers in Israel, led by Shlomo Sharan and Hana Shachar (1988), demonstrated the rapid acceleration of student learning when they studied and first began to use group investigation. These teachers worked with classes in which the children of the poor (referred to as 'low SES', which is shorthand for 'lower socioeconomic status') were mixed with the children of middle class parents (referred to as 'high SES', for 'higher socioeconomic status'). In a year-long course on the social studies, the teachers gave pre-tests of knowledge to the students as well as final examinations, so that they could measure gains in academic learning and compare them with students taught by the 'whole class' format most common in Israeli schools. The results point to several interesting comparisons. First, in the pre-tests the lower SES students scored significantly lower than their higher SES counterparts. (Typically, socioeconomic status is related to the knowledge students bring to the instructional situation, and these students were no exception.) The lower SES students taught by group investigation achieved average gains nearly two and a half times those of the lower SES students taught by the whole-class method *and* exceeded the scores made by the higher SES students taught with the 'whole class' format. In other words, the 'socially disadvantaged' students taught with group investigation learned at rates above those of the 'socially advantaged' students taught by teachers who did not have the repertoire provided by group investigation. Finally, the 'advantaged' students also learned more through group investigation. Their average gain was *twice* that of their whole-class counterparts. Thus the model was effective by a large margin for students from both backgrounds.

Taken as a whole, research on cooperative learning is overwhelmingly positive – nearly every study has had from modest to very high effects. Moreover, cooperative approaches are effective over a range of achievement measures. The more intensely cooperative the environment, the greater the effects; the more complex the outcomes (i.e. higher order processing of information, problem solving), the greater the effects. The cooperative environment engendered by these models has had substantial effects on the cooperative behaviour of students, on increasing feelings of empathy for others, on reducing intergroup tensions and aggressive and antisocial behaviour, on improving moral judgement, and on building positive feelings toward others, including those of other ethnic groups.

REFLECTIONS

Group investigation is a highly versatile and comprehensive model of learning and teaching: it blends the goals of academic inquiry, social integration and social process learning. It can be used in all subject areas, and with all age levels, when the teacher desires to emphasize the formulation and problem solving aspects of knowledge rather than the intake of preorganized, predetermined information. As teachers and researchers who spend much of their time in a wide variety of schools, we were impressed with the maturity of play during break/lunch times at Hempshill Hall school. The children were playing in a far more cooperative and disciplined way than we had seen in other schools. On further investigation we traced this social skill back to the pupils' understanding and internalization of the group investigation model.

Provided that one accepts Thelen's view of knowledge and its reconstruction, the group investigation model can be considered a very direct and efficient way of teaching academic knowledge as well as social process. It also appears likely to nurture interpersonal warmth and trust, respect for negotiated rules and policies, independence in learning, and respect for the dignity of others. Figure 7.1 displays the instructional and nurturant effects, and Table 7.1 the syntax of the group investigation model.

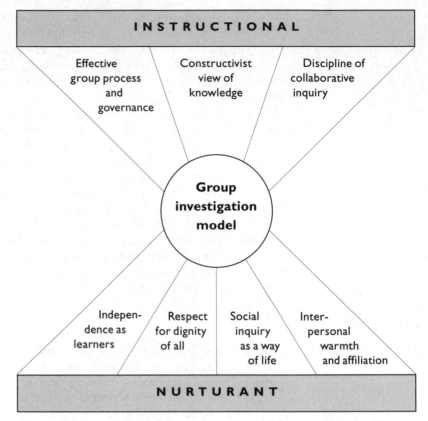

Figure 7.1 Instructional and nurturant effects of the group investigation model

Table 7.1 Syntax of the group investigation model of learning and teaching

---

Phase 1
Students encounter puzzling situation (planned or unplanned).

Phase 2
Students explore reactions to the situation.

Phase 3
Students formulate study task and organize for study (problem definition, role, assignments, etc.).

Phase 4
Independent and group study.

Phase 5
Students analyse progress and process.

Phase 6
Recycle activity.

---

8 Learning to study values

The *analysis* of values is what's important. Playing the roles lets the values become visible if the analysis is right. Understanding that what you do is a living-out of your values starts the inquiry.

Fannie Shaftel to a group of Palo Alto teachers, May 1969

The role playing model is our second example from the social family of models. We use it to illustrate alternative ways of building a learning community in the classroom. In role playing, students explore human relations problems by enacting problem situations and then discussing the enactments. Together, students can explore feelings, attitudes, values and problem solving strategies.

SCENARIO I

We are in the Year 7 class of a middle school in the East End of London. The students have returned to the classroom from a break and are complaining excitedly to one another. Mr Williams, the teacher, asks what the matter is and they all start joining in at once, discussing a series of difficulties throughout the break. Apparently two of the students began to squabble about who was to take the sports equipment outside. Then all of the students argued about what game to play. Next there was a dispute about choosing sides for the games. This included a dispute over whether the girls should be included with the boys or whether they should play separately. The class finally began to play volleyball, but very shortly there was a dispute over a line call, and the game was never completed.

At first Mr Williams displays his displeasure toward the class. He is angry, not simply over the incidents, but because these arguments have been going on since the beginning of the year. At last he says 'OK, we really have to face this problem. You must be as tired of it as I am, and you really are not acting maturely. So we are going to use a technique that we have been using to discuss family problems to approach our own problems right here in this classroom: we're going to use role playing. Now, I want you to divide into groups and try to identify the types of problems that we've been having. Just take today, for example, and outline the problem situations that got us into this fix.'

The students begin with the argument over taking the sports equipment outside, and then outline other arguments. Each is a typical situation that people face all the time and that they must learn to take a stand on. After the separate groups of students have listed their problems, Mr Williams appoints one of the students to lead a discussion in which each group reports the kinds of problem situations that have come up; the groups agree on a half-dozen problems that have consistently bothered the class.

The students then classify the problems according to type. One type concerns the division of labour. A second type deals with deciding principles for selecting teams. A third type focuses on resolving disputes over the particulars of games, such as whether balls have been hit out of bounds, whether players are out or safe, and so on. Mr Williams then assigns one type of problem to each group and asks the groups to describe situations in which the problems come up. When they have done this, the class votes on which problem to start with. The first problem they select is disputes over rules; the actual problem situation they select is the volleyball game in which the dispute over a line call occurred.

The students talk about how the problem situation develops. It begins when a ball is hit close to the boundary line. One team believes it is in, and the other believes it is out of bounds. The students then argue with one another, and the argument goes on so that the game cannot continue.

Several students are selected to enact the situation. Others gather around and are assigned to observe particular aspects of the role playing that follows. Some students are to look for the particulars of how the argument develops. Some are to study one role player and others another, to determine how they handle the situation.

The enactment is spirited. The students select as role players those who have been on opposite sides during the game, and they become as involved in the argument during the role playing as they were during the actual situation. Finally, they are standing in the middle of the room shouting at one another. At this point, Mr Williams calls 'Time!' and asks the students to describe what has gone on.

Everyone is eager to talk. The discussion gradually focuses on how the attitude of the participants prevented any solution of the problem. No one was listening to the other person, and no one was dealing with the problem of how to resolve honest disputes. Mr Williams asks the students to suggest other ways that people could behave in this kind of conflict. Some students suggest giving in gracefully. But others object that if someone believes he or she is right, that is not an easy thing to do. Finally, the students identify an important question to focus on: 'How can we develop a policy about who should make calls, and how should others feel about those calls?' They decide to re-enact the scene by having all the participants assume that the defensive team should make the calls only when they see clear evidence that a ball is out and the other team has not seen the evidence.

The enactment takes place. This time the players attempt to follow the policy that the defensive team has the right to make the call, but the offensive team has the right to object to a call. Once again, the enactment results in a shouting match; however, after it is over, the students who have watched the enactment point out that the role players have not behaved as if there is a resolution to the situation. They recognize that if there are to be games, there has to be agreement about who can make calls and a certain amount of trust on both sides.

They decide to try a third enactment, this time with two new role players inserted as dispute referees. The introduction of referees completely changes the third enactment. The referees insist that the other players pay attention to them, which the players do not want to do. In discussing this enactment, the students point out that there has to be a system to ensure reasonable order and the resolution of disputes. The students also agree that as things stand, they probably are unable to resolve disputes without including a referee of some sort, but that no referees will be effective unless the students agree to accept the referees' decisions as final. They finally decide that in future games two students will be referees. Those students will be chosen by lottery prior to the game; their function will be to arbitrate and to make all calls relevant to the rules of the game, and their decisions will be final. The students agree that they will see how that system works.

The next day Mr Williams opens up the second set of issues, and the students repeat this process. The exploration of other areas of dispute continues over the next few weeks. At first, many of the notions that are clarified are simply practical ones about how to solve specific problems. Gradually, however, Mr Williams directs the discussion to a consideration of the basic values governing individual behaviour. The students begin to see the problems of communal living; and they develop policies for governing their own behaviour, as individuals and as a group. They also begin to develop skills in negotiating. The students who were locked in conflict gradually learn that if they behave in a slightly different way, others may also modify their behaviour, and problems become easier to solve.

ROLE PLAYING AS A MODEL OF LEARNING AND TEACHING

Role playing as a model of teaching has roots in both the personal and social dimensions of education, because it attempts both to help individuals find personal meaning within their social worlds and to resolve personal dilemmas with the assistance of the social group. In the social dimension, it allows individuals to work together in analysing social situations, especially interpersonal problems, and in developing decent and democratic ways of coping with these situations. We have placed role playing in the social family of models because the social group plays such an indispensable part in human development and because of the unique opportunity that role playing offers for resolving interpersonal and social dilemmas. Several teams of researchers have experimented with role playing, and their treatments of the strategy are remarkably similar. The version we explore here was formulated by Fannie and George Shaftel (1967). We have also incorporated ideas from the work of Mark Chesler and Robert Fox (1966).

On its simplest level, role playing is dealing with problems through action: a problem is delineated, acted out and discussed. Some students are role players, others observers. A person puts himself or herself in the position of another person and then tries to interact with others who are also playing roles. As empathy, sympathy, anger and affection are all generated during the interaction, role playing, if done well, becomes a part of life. This emotional content, as well as the words and the actions, becomes part of the later analysis. When the acting out is finished, even the observers are involved enough to want to know why each person reached his or her decision, what the sources of resistance were, and whether there were other ways to approach this situation.

The essence of role playing is the involvement of participants and observers in a real problem situation, and the desire for resolution and understanding that this involvement engenders. The role playing process provides a live sample of human behaviour that serves as a vehicle for students to:

• explore their feelings;
• gain insight into their attitudes, values and perceptions;
• develop their problem solving skills and attitudes; and
• explore subject matter in varied ways.

These goals reflect several assumptions about the learning process in role playing. First, role playing implicitly advocates an experience-based learning situation in which the 'here and now' becomes the content of instruction. The model assumes that it is possible to create authentic analogies to real-life problem situations and that through these re-creations students can 'sample' life. Thus the enactment elicits genuine, typical emotional responses and behaviours from the students.

A related assumption is that role playing can draw out students' feelings, which they can recognize and perhaps release. The Shaftels' version of role playing emphasizes the intellectual content as much as the emotional content; analysis and discussion of the enactment are as important as the role playing itself. We, as educators, are concerned that students recognize and understand their feelings and see how their feelings influence their behaviour.

Another assumption is that emotions and ideas can be brought to consciousness and enhanced by the group. The collective reactions of the peer group can bring out new ideas and provide directions for growth and change. The model de-emphasizes the traditional role of teacher and encourages listening and learning from one's peers.

A final assumption is that covert psychological processes involving one's own attitudes, values and belief system can be brought to consciousness by combining spontaneous enactment with analysis. Furthermore, individuals can gain some measure of control over their belief systems if they recognize their values and attitudes and test them against the views of others. Such analysis can help them evaluate their attitudes and values and the consequences of their beliefs, so that they can allow themselves to grow.

THE CONCEPT OF ROLE

Each individual has a unique manner of relating to people, situations and objects. One person may feel that most people are dishonest and cannot be trusted; someone else may feel that everyone is interesting and may look forward to meeting new people. People also evaluate and behave in consistent ways toward themselves, seeing themselves as powerful and smart, or perhaps afraid and not very able. These feelings about people and situations and about themselves influence people's behaviour and determine how they will respond in various situations. Some people respond with aggressive and hostile behaviour, playing the part of a bully. Others withdraw and remain alone, playing the part of a shy or sulking person.

These parts people play are called *roles*. A role is a 'patterned sequence of feelings, words, and actions . . . It is a unique and accustomed manner of relating to others' (Chesler and Fox 1966; 5, 8). Unless people are looking for them, it is sometimes hard to perceive consistencies and patterns in behaviour. But they are usually there. Terms such as *friendly*, *bully*, *snob*, *know-it-all* and *grouch* are convenient for describing characteristic responses and roles.

The roles individuals play are determined by several factors over many years. The kinds of people someone meets determine his or her general feelings about people. How those people act toward the individual and how the individuals perceive their feelings toward them influence their feelings about themselves. The rules of one's particular culture and institutions help determine which roles a person assumes and how he or she plays them.

People may not be happy with the roles they have assumed. And they may misperceive the attitudes and feelings of others because they do not recognize *their* role and *why* they play it. Two people can share the same feelings but behave in very different ways. They can desire the same goals, but if one person's behaviour is misperceived by others, he or she may not attain that goal.

For a clear understanding of oneself and of others, it is thus extremely important that a person be aware of roles and how they are played. To do this, each person must be able to put himself or herself in another's place, and to experience as much as possible that person's thoughts and feelings. If someone is able to empathize, he or she can accurately interpret social events and interactions. Role playing is a vehicle that forces people to take the roles of others.

The concept of role is one of the central theoretical underpinnings of the role playing model. It is also a major goal. We must teach students to use this concept, to recognize different roles, and to think of their own and others' behaviour in terms of roles. At the same time there are many other aspects to this model, and many levels of analysis, which to some extent compete with one another. For example, the content of the problem, the solutions to the problem, the feelings of the role players and the acting itself all serve to involve students in the role play. Therefore, to be a salient part of the role playing experience, the concept of role must be interwoven yet kept in the fore throughout all the role playing activities. It also helps if, prior to using the model, students have been taught this concept directly.

PHASES OF THE MODEL

The Shaftels suggest that the role playing activity consists of nine steps:

1 warm up the group,
2 select participants,
3 set the stage,
4 prepare observers,
5 enact,
6 discuss and evaluate,
7 re-enact,
8 discuss and evaluate, and
9 share experiences and generalize.

Each of these steps or phases has a specific purpose that contributes to the richness and focus of the learning activity. Together they ensure that a line of thinking is pursued throughout the complex of activities, that students are prepared in their roles, that goals for the role play are identified, and that the discussion afterward is not simply a collection of diffuse reactions, though these are important too.

As a brief review: in the classroom, the role playing model begins with a scenario of a problem or experience with a problem (as in Scenario 1). It proceeds to an analysis of the nature of the encounters in which the problem emerges. Then enactments with observations are followed by analyses of the value positions that are elicited through the enactment. Successive enactments and analyses gradually surface the value positions and lead the students toward policy.

RESEARCH

The benefits of role playing depend on the quality of the enactment and especially on the analysis that follows. They depend also on the students' perceptions of the role as similar to real-life situations. Children do not necessarily engage effectively in role playing or role analysis the first time they try it. Many have to learn to engage in role playing in a sincere way so that the content generated can be analysed seriously.

Chesler and Fox (1966: 64–6) suggest pantomimic exercises as a way of freeing inexperienced students. Role playing is not likely to be successful if the teacher simply tosses out a problem situation, persuades a few children to act it out, and then conducts a discussion about the enactment.

REFLECTIONS

Role playing is designed specifically to foster:

1 the analysis of personal values and behaviour;
2 the development of strategies for solving interpersonal (and personal) problems; and
3 the development of empathy toward others.

Its nurturants are the acquisition of information about social problems and values, comfort in expressing one's opinions, and an integrative social environment. Figure 8.1 displays the instructional and nurturant effects of the role play model of teaching. Table 8.1 summarizes the phases and activities of the model.

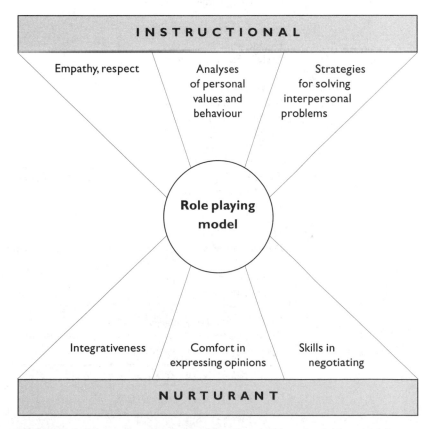

Figure 8.1 Instructional and nurturant effects of the role playing model

Role playing, as do the other social models, draws on the energy of the group; it capitalizes on common cause and the potential that comes from differing points of view and orientations. In Hempshill Hall school, teachers use this model to help students learn to work together to identify and solve problems.

Table 8.1 Syntax of the role playing model of learning and teaching

Phase 1: warm up the group
Identify or introduce problem.
Make problem explicit.
Interpret problem story, explore issues.
Explain role playing.

Phase 2: select participants
Analyse roles.
Select role players.

Phase 3: set the stage
Set line of action.
Restate roles.
Get inside problem situation.

Phase 4: prepare the observers
Decide what to look for.
Assign observation tasks.

Phase 5: enact
Begin role play.
Maintain role play.
Break role play.

Phase 6: discuss and evaluate
Review action of role play (events, position, realism).
Discuss major focus.
Develop next enactment.

Phase 7: re-enact
Play revise roles; suggest next steps or behavioural alternatives.

Phase 8: discuss and evaluate
As in phase 6.

Phase 9: share experiences and generalize
Relate problem situation to real experience and current problems.
Explore general principles of behaviour.

Source: based on Shaftel and Shaftel (1967)

9 Learning through counselling

The idea that you teach kids how to ask and answer questions, rather than just asking them questions, came as a revelation to me.

A teacher of 20 years, to Bruce Joyce, May 1995

From the personal family of models of learning and teaching, we have selected Carl Rogers' nondirective model to illustrate the philosophy and techniques of the personal family and to deal with the organization of the classroom as a self-disciplining community of learners. Let's look first at the nondirective model being used with a whole class as a unit.

SCENARIO I

One of the important uses of nondirective teaching occurs when a class becomes 'stale' and the teacher finds himself or herself just 'pushing' the students through exercises and subject matter. Jane Goring, a middle school teacher exhausted by the failure of more traditional attempts to cope with the discipline problems and the lack of interest on the part of her class, decided to experiment with student-centred teaching. She turned to nondirective approaches to help her students take more responsibility for their learning and to ensure that the subject matter would be related to their needs and learning styles. She has provided an account of that experience, from which excerpts are presented here.

5 March, we begin
A week ago I decided to initiate a new programme in my classroom, based on student-centred teaching – an unstructured or non-directive approach.

I began by telling the class that we were going to try an 'experiment'. I explained that for one day I would let them do anything they wanted to do – they did not have to do anything if they did not want to.

Many students started with art projects; some drew or painted for most of the day. Others read or did work in maths and other

subjects. There was an air of excitement all day. Many were so interested in what they were doing that they did not want to go out at
break!

At the end of the day, I asked the class to evaluate the experiment.
The comments were most interesting. Some were 'confused', dis-
tressed without the teacher telling them what to do, without specific
assignments to complete.

The majority of the class thought the day was 'great', but some
expressed concern over the noise level and the fact that a few students 'messed around' all day. Most felt that they had accomplished
as much work as we usually do, and they enjoyed being able to work
at a task until it was completed, without the pressure of a time limit.
They liked doing things without being 'forced' to do them and liked
deciding what to do.

They begged to continue the 'experiment', so it was decided to do
so, for two more days. We could then re-evaluate the plan.

The next morning, I implemented the idea of a 'work contract'. I
gave them worksheets listing all our subjects with suggestions for
activities or accomplishments under each. There was a space provided for their 'plans' in each area and for comments on completion.

Each child was to write his or her contract for the day – choosing
the areas in which to work and planning specifically what to do. On
completion of any exercise, drill, review, etc., the student was to
check and correct his or her own work, using the teacher's manual.
The work was to be kept in a folder with the contract.

I met with each child to discuss his or her plans. Some completed
theirs in a very short time; we discussed as a group what this might
mean, and what to do about it. It was suggested that the plan might
not be challenging enough, that an adjustment should be made –
perhaps going on or adding another idea to the day's plan.

Resource materials were provided, suggestions made, and drill
materials made available to use when needed.

I found I had much more time, so I worked, talked and spent the
time with individuals and groups. At the end of the third day, I evaluated the work folder with each child. To solve the problem of assessment, I had each child tell me what he or she had learned.

12 March, progress report
Our 'experiment' has, in fact, become our programme – with some
adjustments.

Some children continued to be frustrated and felt insecure without
teacher direction. Discipline also continued to be a problem with
some; and I began to realize that, although some of the children may
need the programme more than others, I was expecting too much
from them, too soon – they were not ready to assume self-direction
yet. Perhaps a gradual weaning from the spoon-fed procedures was
necessary.

I regrouped the class – creating two groups. The largest group is the nondirected. The smallest is teacher-directed, made up of children who wanted to return to the former teacher-directed method, and those who, for varied reasons, were unable to function in the self-directed situation. I would have waited longer to see what would happen, but the situation for some disintegrated a little more each day – penalizing the whole class. The disrupting factor kept everyone upset and limited those who wanted to study and work. So it seemed to me best for the group as a whole, as well as the programme, to modify the plan.

Those who continued the 'experiment' have forged ahead. I showed them how to design or 'programme' their work, using their texts as a basic guide. They have learned that they can teach themselves (and each other), and that I am available when a step is not clear or advice is needed.

At the end of each week, they evaluate themselves in each area – in terms of work accomplished, accuracy, progress toward long-term goals, etc. We have learned that the number of errors is not a criterion of failure or success, for errors can and should be part of the learning process. We also discussed the fact that consistently perfect scores may mean that the work is not challenging enough and perhaps we should move on.

After self-evaluation, each child brings the evaluation sheet and work folder to discuss with me.

Some of the members of the group working with me are most anxious to become 'independent' students. We evaluate together each week their progress toward that goal.

Some students (there were two or three) who originally wanted to return to the teacher-directed programme are now anticipating going back into the self-directed programme. (I sense that it has been as difficult for them to readjust to the old programme as it would be for me to do so.)

Let us now look at the nondirective model being used with an individual student.

SCENARIO 2

Ray Bolam, a 26-year-old secondary school English teacher in Sheffield, is very concerned about Sue Fortnay, one of his students. Sue is a compulsive worker who does an excellent job with literature assignments and writes excellent short stories. She is, however, reluctant to share those stories with other members of the class and declines to participate in any activities in the performing arts.

Mr Bolam recognizes that the issue cannot be forced, but he wants Sue to understand why she is reluctant to allow any public display of her talents. She will make her own decisions about participation that involves sharing her ideas.

One afternoon she asks him to read some of her pieces and give her his opinion.

Sue: 'Mr Bolam, could you take a look at these for me?'

Bolam: 'Certainly, Sue. Another short story?'

Sue: 'No, some poems I've been working on. I don't think they're very good, but I'd like you to tell me what you think.'

Bolam: 'When did you write them?'

Sue: 'One Sunday afternoon a couple of weeks ago.'

Bolam: 'Do you remember what started you thinking that you wanted to write a poem?'

Sue: 'I was feeling sort of sad and I remembered last month when we tried to read *The Waste Land*, and it seemed to be trying to say a lot of things that we couldn't say in the usual way. I liked the beginning lines, 'April is the cruellest month, breeding lilacs out of the dead land.'

Bolam: 'And this is what you wrote down?'

Sue: 'Yes. It's the first time I've ever tried writing anything like this.'

Bolam (reads for a few minutes, then looks up): 'Sue, these are really good.'

Sue: 'What makes a poem good, Mr Bolam?'

Bolam: 'Well, there are a variety of ways to judge poetry. Some methods are technical and have to do with the quality of expression and the way one uses metaphors and analogies and other literary devices. Others are subjective and involve the quality of expression, the real beauty of the words themselves.'

Sue: 'I felt very good when I was writing them, but when I read them over, they sound stupid to me.'

Bolam: 'What do you mean?'

Sue: 'Oh, I don't know. I guess the main thing is that I feel ashamed if anybody else sees them.'

Bolam: 'Ashamed?'

Sue: 'I really don't know. I just know that if these were to be read aloud, say to my class, I would be so embarrassed.'

Bolam: 'You really feel that the class would laugh at these?'

Sue: 'Oh yeah, they wouldn't understand.'

Bolam: 'How about your short stories? How do you feel about them?'

Sue: 'You know I don't want *anybody* to see what I write.'

Bolam: 'You really feel that you want to put them away somewhere so nobody can see them?'

Sue: 'Yes, I really think so. I don't know exactly why, but I'm pretty sure that no one in my class would understand them.'

Bolam: 'Can you think of anybody else that might understand them?'

Sue: 'I don't know. I suppose there are people out there who might, but nobody around here, probably.'

Bolam: 'How about your parents?'

Sue: 'Oh, they like everything I write.'

Bolam: 'Well, that makes three of us. Can you think of anybody else?'

Sue: 'I guess I think adults would, but I'm not really so sure about other people my age.'

Bolam: 'Are people your age somehow different from adults in this respect?'

Sue: 'Well, they just don't seem to be interested in these kinds of things. I feel they put down anybody who tries to write anything.'

Bolam: 'Do you think they feel this way about the authors we read in class?'

Sue: 'Well, sometimes they do, but I guess a lot of the time they really enjoy the stories.'

Bolam: 'Well then, why do you think they wouldn't like what you write?'

Sue: 'I guess I don't really know, Mr Bolam. I guess I'm really afraid, but I can't put my finger on it.'

Bolam: 'Something holds you back.'

Sue: 'In a lot of ways, I really would like to find out whether anybody would appreciate what I write. I just don't know how to go about it.'

Bolam: 'How would you feel if I were to read one of your short stories but not tell them who wrote it?'

Sue: 'Would you promise?'

Bolam: 'Of course I would. Then we could talk about how everybody reacted. You would know that they didn't know who had written it.'

Sue: 'I don't know, but it sounds interesting.'

Bolam: 'Depending on what happened, we could cook up some kind of strategy about what to do next.'

Sue: 'Well, I guess I don't have much to lose.'

Bolam: 'I hope we're always where you don't have anything to lose, Sue; but there's always a risk in telling about ourselves.'

Sue: 'What do you mean, telling about ourselves?'

Bolam: 'I have to go now – but let me pick one of your stories and read it next week, and then let's get together on Wednesday and talk about what happened.'

Sue: 'OK, and you promise not to tell?'

Bolam: 'I promise. I'll see you next Wednesday after school.'

Sue: 'OK. Thanks a lot, Mr Bolam. Have a good weekend.'

THE NONDIRECTIVE MODEL OF LEARNING AND TEACHING

Both Jane Goring and Ray Bolam were using the nondirective model of learning and teaching based on the work of psychologist and counsellor Carl Rogers (1961, 1982) and other advocates of nondirective counselling. Rogers believed that positive human relationships enable people to grow; instruction, therefore, should be based on concepts of human relations in contrast to concepts of subject matter. Basically, he extended to education his view of therapy as a mode of learning.

For almost five decades, Carl Rogers was the acknowledged spokesperson for models in which the teacher plays the role of counsellor. Developed from counselling theory, the nondirective model emphasizes a partnership between students and teacher. The teacher endeavours to help the students understand how to play major roles in directing their own education – for example, by behaving in such a way as to clarify goals and participate in developing avenues for reaching those goals. The teacher provides information about how much progress is being made and helps the students solve problems. The nondirective teacher has actively to build the partnerships that are required and provide the help needed as students try to work out their problems.

As with other models in the personal family, the nondirective model has the following purposes:

- to lead the student toward greater mental and emotional health by developing self-confidence, forming a realistic sense of self and building empathetic reactions to others;
- to increase the proportion of education that emanates from the needs and aspirations of the student – that is, taking each student as a partner in determining what he or she will learn and how he or she will learn it;
- to develop speciWc kinds of qualitative thinking, such as creativity and personal expression.

Rogerian teaching is an emergent, 'rolling' model rather than a linear one. It advocates the following of principles rather than scripts when working with students, and the principles create the structure by guiding our interactions. The model can be used with any other model of teaching, or to counsel a group or an individual.

When used in the context of another model, Rogerian principles can guide our behaviour as we help students reach out to learn and reach out to one another. Thus in any teaching/learning encounter we can behave so as to:

- radiate warmth and confidence to the students;
- radiate empathy and understanding;
- help the students understand how their stance toward tasks and others can draw them toward self-actualization.

When counselling, we add the dimensions of:

- helping the students clarify a general or specific problem;
- helping the students take responsibility for changing their behaviour so as to solve the problem;
- helping the students experiment and reflect on the results of their experimentation;
- helping them develop empathy toward others in their environment.

PHASES OF THE MODEL

Despite the fluidity and unpredictability of the nondirective strategy, Rogers points out that the nondirective interview has a sequence. In the nondirective model of teaching we have divided this sequence into five phases of activity. Think about the scenarios and examples presented above as you read the description of each phase.

In *phase 1* the helping situation is defined. This includes structuring remarks by the counsellor that define the student's freedom to express feelings, an agreement on the general focus of the interview, an initial problem statement, some discussion of the relationship if it is to be ongoing, and the establishment of procedures for meeting. Phase 1 generally occurs during the initial session on a problem. However, some structuring or definition by the teacher may be necessary for some time, even if this consists only of occasional summarizing moves that redefine the problem and reflect progress. Naturally these structuring and definitional comments vary considerably with the type of interview, the specific problem and the student.

In *phase 2* the student is encouraged by the teacher's acceptance and clarification to express negative and positive feelings, to state and explore the problem.

In *phase 3* the student gradually develops insight: he or she perceives new meaning in his or her experiences, sees new relationships of cause and effect, and understands the meaning of his or her previous behaviour. In most situations, the student seems to alternate between exploring the problem itself and developing new insight into his or her feelings. Both activities are necessary for progress. Discussion of the problem without exploration of feelings would indicate that the student him- or herself was being avoided.

In *phase 4* the student moves toward planning and decision making with respect to the problem. The role of the teacher is to clarify the alternatives.

In *phase 5* the student reports the actions he or she has taken, develops further insight and plans increasingly more integrated and positive actions.

These five phases could occur in one session or, more likely, over a series. In the latter case, phases 1 and 2 could occur in the first few discussions, phases 3 and 4 in the next, and phase 5 in the last interview. Or, if the encounter consists of a voluntary meeting with a student who has an immediate problem, phases 1 through 4 could occur in only one meeting, with the student returning briefly to report his or her actions and insights. On the other hand, the sessions involved in negotiating academic contracts are sustained for a period of time, and the context of each meeting generally involves some kind of planning and decision making, although several sessions devoted entirely to exploring a problem might occur.

RESEARCH

Over the years, the nondirective model has been used with all types of students and across all subjects and teaching roles. Although it is designed to promote self-understanding and independence, it has fared well as a contributor to a wide range of academic objectives.

While enhancing the learner as a person is a worthwhile educational goal in its own right, a major thesis of the nondirective model of teaching is that better-developed, more affirmative, self-actualizing learners have increased learning capabilities. This thesis is supported by a number of studies indicating that teachers who incorporate personal models into their repertoires increased achievement among their students (Roebuck *et al.* 1976).

REFLECTIONS

Since the activities and content that compose each phase are not prescribed but are determined by the student as he or she interacts with the teacher and other students, the nondirective teaching model depends largely on its nurturant effects rather than its immediate instructional effects. Its instructional effects are primarily dependent on its success in nurturing more effective self-development. Thus this model can be thought of as entirely nurturant in character, dependent for effects on experiencing the nondirective learning environment rather than on developing specific academic content and skills. In

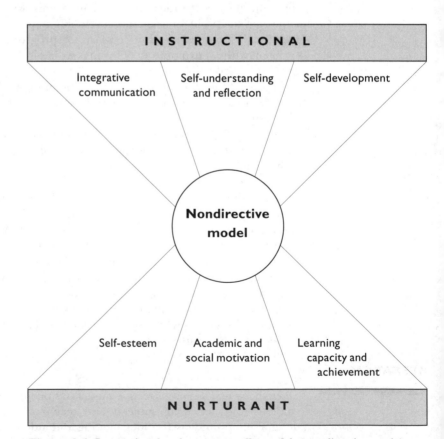

Figure 9.1 Instructional and nurturant effects of the nondirective model

Hempshill Hall this model was not apparent in all its phases, except with some of the older students. Having said that, the first phase of the model – 'the teacher encourages free expression of feelings' – was apparent in all classes and was an important aspect of the school's social climate. In individual and group discussions the children were fluent and confident in talking about their feelings. Figure 9.1 displays the instructional and nurturant effects of the nondirective learning and teaching model; Table 9.1 shows the main phases.

Table 9.1 Syntax of the nondirective model of learning and teaching (individuals)

Phase 1: defining the helping situation
The teacher encourages free expression of feelings.

Phase 2: exploring the problem
The student is encouraged to define the problem.
The teacher accepts and clarifies the student's feelings.

Phase 3: developing insight
The student discusses the problem.
The teacher supports the student.

Phase 4: planning and decision making
The student plans initial decision making
The teacher clarifies possible decisions.

Phase 5: integration
The student gains further insight and develops more positive actions.
The teacher is supportive.

Action outside the interview
The student initiates positive actions.

---

10 Learning through simulations

This is a lot better than turning a real chopper upside down.

Army instructor to Bruce Joyce, June 1953

From the behavioural systems family, we have selected simulation as our illustrative model. In this chapter, we briefly explore the principles of simulation and discuss examples of various kinds of simulations.

SCENARIO 1

In a school in Moscow, a primary class is watching a television screen. The programme announcer portrays a countdown as a rocket attempts to break free from the gravity of the moon but fails to do so. Class members then take the role of members of the spaceship crew. Instructions from the Russian Space Administration divide them into teams, and they prepare to work together to conserve their life support systems and to manage their relationships in the rocket ship until repairs can be made.

SCENARIO 2

In another classroom, this time in the suburbs of Edinburgh, a class is watching a television show. The actors are portraying the members of the Scottish Parliament facing a crisis. After examining the issues, the class reaches a conclusion. One student reaches for the telephone in the classroom, dials a number and speaks to the actors in the studio, suggesting how they might play their roles differently to resolve the crisis. Twenty-five other classrooms are simultaneously debating the issues seen on television and they, too, are communicating their views to the actors in the studio. The next day the show resumes. In various ways, the actors play out the suggestions made by the classes. The other members of the Cabinet react. Students in the 25 classrooms not only see their ideas brought to life on the television screen, they also see the consequences of their recommendations.

SCENARIO 3

In a London school, two groups of children enter a room. One group represents the Alzoa culture, the other the Betam culture. Their task is to learn how to communicate with others who have learned rules and patterns of behaviour from a different society. Gradually they learn to master communication patterns. Simultaneously they become aware that, as members of a culture, they have inherited powerful patterns that strongly influence their personalities and their ways of communicating with other people.

SCENARIO 4

In Livingston, Montana, a class is engaged in a caribou hunt. As they progress through the hunt, which the Netsilik Eskimos operate, they learn behaviour patterns of the Netsilik and begin to compare those patterns with the ones they carry on in their everyday lives.

SCENARIO 5

In Lancaster, a group of students faces a problem posed by the Minister of Agriculture. Agronomists have developed a nutrient that, when added to the food of cattle, greatly increases their weight. Only a limited amount of this nutrient is available, and the students must determine how the nutrient will be divided among the needy countries of the world. The Minister has imposed the following restraints: recipient countries must have a reasonable supply of beef cattle, must not be aligned with support for terrorist organizations, must not be vegetarians, and must have a population that exceeds a certain size.

The students debate the alternatives. Some countries are ruled out immediately. Of the remaining countries, some seem attractive at first, yet less attractive later. The students grapple with the problems of humanity and ideology and with practical situations. In this simulation, they face the problems of the committees of scientists who continually advise Parliament on various courses of action.

SCENARIO 6

There are now a number of computer-based games that make it possible to individualize the simulation in terms of learning pace, scope, sequence and difficulty of material. Aside from this feature, the properties of the simulation remain the same as in noncomputer-based simulation games.

The Sumerian Game (developed by the Center for Educational Services and Research, Board of Cooperative Educational Services, 42 Triangle Center, Yorktown Heights, NY 10598, USA) instructs the student in the basic principles of economics as applied to three stages of a primitive economy – the prevalence of agriculture, the development of crafts, and the introduction of trade and other changes. The game is set during the time of the Neolithic revolution in Mesopotamia, about 3500 BC. The student is asked to take the role of the ruler of the city state of Lagash. The ruler must make certain agricultural decisions for the kingdom at each six-month harvest. For example, the ruler is presented with the following problematic situation: 'We have harvested 5,000 bushels of grain to take care of 500 people. How much of this grain will be set aside for next season's planting and how much will be stored in a warehouse?' (Boocock and Schild 1968: 156). The student is asked to decide how much grain to allocate for consumption, for production and for storage.

These situations become more complex as the game continues, for the student must take into account such circumstances as changes in population, the acquisition of new land and irrigation. Periodically, technological innovations and disasters alter the outcome of the ruler's decisions. The effect of each decision on the economic condition of the kingdom is shown in an immediate progress report. Students are apprised of certain quantitative changes – for example, in population, in the amount of harvested grain and in the amount of stored grain – and they are furnished with some substantive analyses of their decisions, for instance 'The quantity of food the people received last season was far too little' (Boocock and Schild 1968: 164). In phase 2 of the Sumerian Game, the student can apply his or her surplus grain to the development of arts and crafts.

SCENARIO 7

Harold Guetzkow and his associates have developed a very complex and interesting simulation for teaching secondary and high school students the principles of international relations (Guetzkow *et al.* 1963). This international simulation consists of five 'nation' units. In each of these nations, a group of participants acts as decision makers and 'aspiring decision makers'. The simulated relations among the nations are derived from the characteristics of nations and from principles that have been observed to operate among nations in the past. Each of the decision making teams has available to it information about the country it represents. This information concerns the basic capability of the national economic systems, the consumer capability, force capability (the ability of the nation to develop military goods and services), and trade and aid information. Together, the nations play an international relations game that involves trading and the development of various agreements. International organizations can be established, for example, or mutual aid or trade agreements made. The nations can even make war on one another, the outcome being determined by the force capability of one group of allies relative to that of another group.

As students play the roles of national decision makers, they must make realistic negotiations such as those diplomats and other representatives make as nations interact with one another, and they must refer to the countries' economic conditions as they do so. In the course of this game-type simulation, the students learn ways in which economic restraints operate on a country. For example, if they are members of the decision making team of a small country and try to engage in a trade agreement, they find that they have to give something to get something. If their country has a largely agricultural economy and they are dealing with an industrialized nation, they find that their country is in a disadvantageous position unless the other nation badly needs the product they have to sell. By receiving feedback about the consequences of their decision, the students come to an understanding of the principles that operate in international relations.

SIMULATION AS A MODEL OF LEARNING AND TEACHING

The seven scenarios above describe simulations. Elements of the 'real world' have been simplified and presented in a form that can be contained inside a classroom, workroom or living room. The attempt is to simulate realistic conditions as much as possible so that the concepts learned and problem-solutions generated are transferable to the real world and to understanding and performing tasks related to the content of the simulation.

Most simulations are constructed from descriptions of real-life situations, although modified for teaching purposes. Sometimes the renditions are quite elaborate (for example, flight and space flight simulators or simulations of international relations). The student engages in activity to achieve the goal of the simulation (to get the aircraft off the ground, perhaps, or to redevelop an urban area) and has to deal with realistic factors until the goal is mastered.

To progress through the tasks of the simulation, students must develop concepts and skills necessary for performance in the specified area. In the simulations described above, the young caribou hunters have to learn concepts about a certain culture, or the young members of the Cabinet need to learn about international relations and the problems of governing a nation. Students also learn from the consequences of their actions. The students who do poorly in the caribou hunt learn what happens if the culture does not function efficiently, or if its members shrink from carrying out the tasks that enable them to survive.

Some simulations are games, some not; some are competitive, some cooperative; and some are played by individuals against their own standard. For example, competition is important in the familiar board game, Monopoly. Monopoly simulates the activity of real-estate speculators and incorporates many elements of real-life speculation. The winning player learns the 'rules' of investment and speculation as embodied in the game.

In simulations such as the Life Career game, players attempt to reach their goals in a noncompetitive way. No score is kept, but interactions are recorded and analysed later. In the Life Career game, the students play out the life cycle of a human being: they select mates, choose careers, decide whether to obtain various amounts of education, and learn (through the consequences of their decisions) how these choices can affect their lives.

In the familiar computer simulations like Sim City and Sim Earth, students can play alone or together against their own standard for creating a good quality of life.

Nearly all simulations depend on *software* – that is, materials or paraphernalia of various kinds, from the driving simulator in the scenario above; to the information and materials about the life of Netsilik Eskimos; to the Monopoly board, money, and symbols of property; to the computer and computer software program of Sim Earth.

Effective use of the simulation model in the classroom depends on how the teacher blends the already prepared simulation into the curriculum, highlighting and reinforcing the learning inherent in the game. Both the teacher's ability to make the activities truly meaningful and the self-instructional property of simulations are vital.

Computers and simulations

In the immediate future, the personal computer and an abundance of software are going to greatly increase the likelihood that simulations will be used in schools. Sorting out from the developing storehouse of software those items that will be useful is not easy and is worth a few words here.

The currently available software can be loosely divided into three categories:

1 games built around fantasy adventures,
2 game-like simulations that tangentially involve curriculum-relevant content, and
3 simulations developed to accomplish educational purposes.

Fantasy adventures are not designed to teach real-life concepts and skills, but they do require logical thinking and may well promote it. Working one's way through Middle Earth or working through the levels of Dungeons and Dragons can certainly encourage logical thinking.

Game-like simulations, like the Carmen San Diego Series, involving puzzles set in real-life terrain – such as the United States, Europe, or a period in history – are not designed to teach geographical or historical concepts, but may well add to knowledge. Following the Carmen San Diego gang around the world will acquaint the player with information about our world, its geography and its economy, although not in depth.

Simulations that require learning academic concepts can be an important part of a curriculum. Examples in the Sim series include Sim City, where students construct communities and have to face the consequences of decisions. For instance they learn that saving land for parks means a lessening of areas for residential, commercial or industrial use, balanced against quality-of-living considerations. When assessing software, finding simulations that require the learning and application of academic concepts should be a high priority.

PHASES OF THE MODEL

The simulation model has four phases: orientation, participant training, the simulation itself and debriefing.

During the orientation, *phase 1*, the teacher presents the topic to be explored, the concepts that are embedded in the actual simulation, an explanation of 'simulation' if this is the students' first experience with it, and an overview of the game itself. This first part should not be lengthy but can be an important context for the remainder of the learning activity.

During participant training, *phase 2*, the students begin to get into the simulation. At this point the teacher sets the scenario by introducing the students to the rules, roles, procedures, scoring, types of decisions to be made, and goals of the simulation. He or she organizes the students into the various roles and conducts an abbreviated practice session to ensure that students have understood all the directions and can carry out their roles.

Phase 3 is the participation in the simulation. The students participate in the game or simulation, and the teacher functions in his or her role as referee and coach. Periodically the simulation may be stopped so that the students receive feedback, evaluate their performances and decisions, and clarify any misconceptions.

Finally, *phase 4* consists of participant debriefing. Depending on the outcomes, the teacher may help the students focus on:

- the events and their other perceptions and reactions,
- analysing the process,
- comparing the simulation to the real world,
- relating the activity to course content, and
- appraising and redesigning the simulation.

From the point of view of the teacher, the use of simulations is deceptively simple. The process of debriefing, which surely occurs after each use and may occur periodically throughout the simulation, is the one most often neglected.

RESEARCH

Simulations have been used increasingly in education over the last 30 years, but the simulation model did not originate within the field of education. Rather, it is an application of the principles of *cybernetics*, a branch of psychology. Cybernetic psychologists, making an analogy between humans and machines, conceptualize the learner as a self-regulating feedback system. The central focus is the apparent similarity between the feedback control mechanisms of electromechanical system and human systems. 'A feedback control system incorporates three primary functions: it generates movement of the system toward a target or defined path; it compares the effects of this action with the true path and detects error; and it utilizes this error signal to redirect the system' (Smith and Smith 1966: 203).

For example, the automatic pilot of a boat continually corrects the helm of the ship, depending on the readings of the compass. When the ship begins to swing in a certain direction and the compass moves off the desired heading more than a certain amount, a motor is switched on and the helm moves over. When the ship returns to its course, the helm straightens out again and the ship continues on its way. The automatic pilot operates in essentially the same way as a human pilot. Both watch the compass, and both move the wheel to the left or right, depending on what is going on. Both initiate action in terms of a specified goal ('Let's go north'), and depending on the feedback or error signal, both redirect the initial action. Very complex self-regulating mechanical systems have been developed to control devices such as guided missiles, ocean liners and satellites.

Cybernetic psychologists interpret the human being as a control system that generates a course of action and then redirects or corrects the action by means of feedback. This can be a very complicated process (as when the Secretary of State re-evaluates foreign policy) or a very simple one (as when we notice that our sailboat is heading into the wind too much and we ease off on our course just a little). In using the analogy of mechanical systems as a frame of reference for analysing human beings, psychologists came up with the central idea 'that performance and learning must be analysed in terms of the control relationships between a human operator and an instrumental situation'. That is, learning was understood to be determined by the nature of the individual, as well as by the design of the learning situation (Smith and Smith 1966: vii).

All human behaviour, according to cybernetic psychology, involves a perceptible pattern of motion. This includes both covert behaviour, such as thinking and symbolic behaviour, and overt behaviour. In any given situation, individuals modify their behaviour according to the feedback they receive from the environment. They organize their movements and their response patterns in relation to this feedback. Thus their own sensorimotor capabilities form the basis of their feedback systems. This ability to receive feedback constitutes the human system's mechanism for receiving and sending information. As human beings develop greater linguistic capability they are able to use indirect as well as direct feedback, thereby expanding their control over the physical and social environment. That is, they are less dependent on the concrete realities of the environment because they can use its symbolic representations.

The essence, then, of cybernetic psychology is the principle of sense-oriented feedback that is intrinsic to the individual (one 'feels' the effects of one's decisions) and is the basis for self-corrective choices. For example, in the driving simulation, if the driver heads into curves too rapidly and then has to jerk the wheel to avoid going off the road, this feedback permits the driver to adjust his or her behaviour so that when driving on a real road he or she will turn more gingerly when approaching sharp curves. The cybernetic psychologist designs simulators so that the feedback about the consequences of behaviour enables the learners to modify their responses and develop a repertoire of appropriate behaviours. According to this view, individuals can 'feel' the effects of their decisions because the environment responds *in full*, rather than simply 'You're right' or 'Wrong! Try again.' That is, the environmental consequences of their choices are played back to them. *Learning* in cybernetic terms is sensorially experiencing the environmental consequences of one's behaviour and engaging in self-corrective behaviour. Instruction in cybernetic terms is designed to create an environment for the learner in which this full feedback takes place.

CODA: SOME TIPS FOR TEACHERS FROM THE BEHAVIOURAL STANCE

Although we have concentrated primarily on simulation, which is only one model from the behavioural systems family, the frame of reference of behavioural psychologists can be used to think about many common classroom events and problems faced by teachers. Here are some examples in the form of questions and tips.

Classroom rules

Which is best, a list of behaviours to avoid and negative reinforcers (a one-time violation results in the 'name on the board', a two-time violation results in 'loss of break', etc.), or a list of desirable behaviours and rewards (a certificate proclaiming 'You are a super student!' 'You are a great reader')?

Tip: the best bet is the positive rules and the positive reinforcers or nurturers.

Off-task behaviour

If 28 students are on-task and two are off-task, which teacher behaviour has the highest probability of succeeding in bringing the two into an on-task mode: reprimanding the off-task students or praising the on-task students?

Tip: praising the on-task students (positive rather than negative reinforcement).

Instruction or self-instruction

In the technology suite, when introducing a new word-processing program to students who can already use another program, one teacher takes the students step by step through the manual. The other teacher gives the students the program and, after a brief orientation, asks them to teach themselves to use the program. Which works best?

Tip: controlling your own learning schedule arouses positive affect. Also pacing is under the control of the individual, who can move rapidly or slowly according to their needs.

Itchy students

A child just doesn't seem to sit still or pay attention for more than a few minutes at a time. Do you: Give the child extra homework when he/she wanders off-task or teach him/her a relaxation exercise and how to use it when the hyperactive feeling rises?

Tip: the first 'solution' is a negative reinforcer that also uses academic work as a punishment, which can produce an aversive response to academic tasks and assignments in general. The second provides effective control, makes the student a partner in regulating his/her behaviour, and provides the opportunity for positive self-reinforcement as well as external reinforcement.

Motivation

Following a test at the end of a unit in mathematics, one teacher has the students correct their own papers and figure out their gain scores. The other teacher scores the tests and provides the students with an analysis of items missed. Which is the best bet for motivating the students?

Tip: self-scoring, emphasis on progress, and setting of new goals will win almost every time.

REFLECTIONS

The simulation model, through the actual activity and through discussions afterwards, provides instruction in and nurtures a variety of educational outcomes including the development of concepts and skills, cooperation and competition, critical thinking and decision making, empathy, knowledge of political/social/economic systems, sense of individual effectiveness, awareness of the role of chance, and facing consequences. Figure 10.1 displays the instructional and nurturant effects of simulations; Table 10.1 summarizes the main phases of the model.

The behavioural stance, from which simulations are derived, is very useful in thinking about certain dimensions of learning. Sometimes behaviourism is stereotyped as overcontrolling and relying on external rewards. We emphasize its usefulness in understanding self-teaching capability, particularly the role of experimenting with behaviour and learning from success and failure. We cannot overemphasize the importance of student capability for self-teaching. Nor can we understate how careful we all need to be to arrange the environment so that we do not inadvertently shape the learner's response away from productive behaviour. For example, we have known teachers of English composition who graded largely on the basis of neatness and correctness of penmanship rather than on the structure of the writing or its imaginativeness.

We are fortunate to have simulations as an available model of learning and teaching, for simulations allow students to experience situations that they cannot realistically experience directly, such as international decision making or urban redevelopment. Simulated experiments in areas such as genetics, physics and chemistry enable students to generate and test hypotheses on topics that simply could not be explored otherwise. Even in a primary or elementary school such as Hempshill Hall, children were deliberately exposed to real-life learning situations early in their school careers. Aspects of school life, such as the dignity and authenticity attached to the provision and purchase of pre-school breakfast, were easily assimilated into and utilized as part of the whole-school experience.

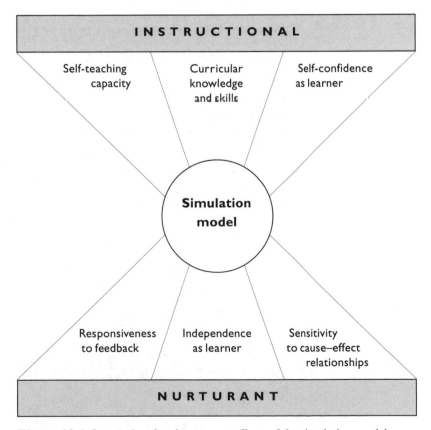

Figure 10.1 Instructional and nurturant effects of the simulation model

Table 10.1 Syntax of the simulation model of learning and teaching

Phase 1: orientation

Present the broad topic of the simulation and the concepts to be incorporated into the simulation activity at hand.

Explain simulation and gaming.

Give overview of the simulation.

Phase 2: participant training

Set up the scenario (rules, roles, procedures, scoring, types of decisions to be made, goals).

Assign roles.

Hold abbreviated practice session.

Phase 3: simulation operations

Conduct game activity and game administration.

Obtain feedback and evaluation (of performance and effects of decisions).

Clarify misconceptions.

Continue simulation.

Phase 4: participant debriefing (any or all of the following activities)

Summarize events and perceptions.

Summarize difficulties and insights.

Analyse process.

Compare simulation activity to the real world.

Relate simulation activity to course content.

Appraise and redesign the simulation.

11 The conditions of learning: integrating models of learning and teaching

Let me conclude with one last point. What I have said suggests that mental growth is in very considerable measure dependent upon growth from the outside in – a mastering of techniques that are embodied in the culture and that are passed on in a contingent dialogue by agents of the culture . . . I suspect that much of growth starts out by our turning around on our own traces and recoding new forms, with the aid of adult tutors, what we have been doing or seeing, then going on to new modes of organisation with the new products that have been formed by these recodings . . . It is this that leads me to think that the heart of the educational process consists of providing aids and dialogues for translating experience into more powerful systems of notation and ordering. And it is for this reason that I think a theory of development must be linked to a theory of knowledge and to a theory of instruction, or be doomed to triviality.

Jerome Bruner (1966: 21)

Planning curricula, courses, units and lessons is a *sine qua non* of good teaching. In this chapter, we study planning with a master and then try to apply his framework to the problem of planning for learning and teaching.

One of the most important books on learning and teaching is Robert N. Gagné's *Conditions of Learning* (1965). Gagné gives us a careful analysis of the important variables in learning and how to organize teaching to take these variables into account. His picture of the 'varieties of chance called learning' enables us to classify and specify learning objectives and the relationships *between* various kinds of learning performances.

VARIETIES OF PERFORMANCE

Gagné identifies six varieties of performances that represent different classes or types of learning:

1 specific responding,
2 chaining,
3 multiple discrimination,
4 classifying,
5 rule using, and
6 problem solving.

Specific responding is making a specific response to a particular stimulus. An example occurs when a Year 1 teacher holds up a card (the stimulus) on which the word *dog* is printed and the children say 'dog' (the response). Specific responding is an extremely important type of learning and is the way we have acquired much of the information we possess. In order for the pupil to learn to make correct, specific responses, we must assume he or she has the ability to make connections between things. In the previous example, the printed word *dog* is associated, or connected, with the verbal statement 'dog'.

Chaining is making a series of responses that are linked together. Gagné uses the example of unlocking a door with a key and of translating from one language to another. Unlocking a door requires us to use a number of specific responses (selecting a key, inserting it, turning it) in an order that will get the job done. When one takes the English words 'How are you?' and translates them to 'Cómo está usted?' in Spanish, one is chaining by taking a series of specific responses and linking them into a phrase.

Multiple discrimination is involved in learning a variety of specific responses and chains, and in learning how to sort them out appropriately. For example, one learns to associate colours with their names under very similar conditions, but then has to sort out the colours and apply them to varieties of objects under different conditions, choosing the right responses and chains. Similarly, when learning a language, one develops a storehouse of words and phrases. When spoken to, one has to sort out the reply, adjusting for gender, number, tense and so forth. Multiple discrimination, then, involves learning to handle previously learned chains of various sorts.

Classifying is assigning objects to classes denoting similar functions. Learning to distinguish plants from animals or cars from bicycles involves classifying. The result of this process is *concepts*, ideas that compare and contrast things and events or describe causal relations among them.

Rule using is the ability to act on a concept that implies action. For example, in spelling we learn varieties of concepts that describe how words are spelled. Then we apply those concepts in rule form in the act of spelling itself. For example, one learns that in consonant-vowel words ending in *t*, such as *sit*, the consonant is doubled when *ing* is added. This becomes a rule (double the *t*) that one usually follows in spelling such words.

Finally, *problem solving* is the application of several rules to a problem not encountered before by the learner. Problem solving involves selecting the correct rules and applying them in combination. For example, a child learns several rules about balancing on a seesaw and then applies them when moving a heavy object with a lever.

FACILITATING THE SIX CLASSES OF LEARNING

Gagné believes that these six types of learning form an ascending hierarchy: thus, before one can chain, one has to learn specific responses; multiple discrimination requires prior learning of several chains;

classifying builds on multiple discrimination; rules for action are forms of concepts learned through classification and the establishment of causal relations; and problem solving requires previously learned rules.

Certain conditions are necessary for the development of each class of learning. The task of the teacher is to create these conditions in the classroom. One way of doing this is by using the appropriate model of teaching.

Let's look now at the integration of Gagné's classes with the models of learning and teaching.

To facilitate *specific responding*, a stimulus is presented to the student under conditions that will bring about his or her attention and induce a response closely related in time to the presentation of the stimulus. The response is then reinforced. Thus the teacher may hold up the word *dog*, say 'dog', ask the children to say 'dog', and then smile and say 'good'. A teacher who does this repeatedly increases the probability that pupils will learn to recognize words and be able to emit the sounds associated with the letters. The mnemonic and simulations models are approaches that facilitate specific responding. So too are the first phases of the inductive and concept attainment models, and the data gathering activities in group investigations.

To facilitate the acquisition of *chaining*, a sequence of cues is offered and appropriate responses are induced. A language teacher may say 'How are you?', followed by 'Cómo está usted?', inviting the students to say 'How are you?' and 'Cómo está usted?', the teacher may thus provide sufficient repetition that the students will acquire the chain and achieve fluency. The mnemonics and inductive thinking models are appropriate to helping build chains.

To facilitate *multiple discrimination*, practice with correct and incorrect stimuli is needed so that the students can learn to discriminate. For example, suppose the students are learning the Spanish expressions for 'How are you?', 'Good morning' and 'Hello'; they must learn to discriminate which one to use in a given situation. The teacher provides sets of correct and incorrect stimuli until the students learn the appropriate discrimination. Inductive reasoning and concept attainment models are useful in this process.

Classification is taught by presenting varieties of exemplars and concepts so that the students can gradually learn bases for distinguishing them. Inductive thinking and concept attainment are appropriate.

Rule using is facilitated by inducing the students to recall a concept and then apply it to a variety of specific applications. In the earlier spelling example, pupils recall the rule about doubling the final consonant when adding *ing* and are presented with examples they can practise. Simulations and the application phases of concept attainment and inductive thinking help students move from the identification of concepts to their application.

Problem solving is largely done by the students themselves, because problem situations are unique. It can be facilitated by providing sets of problems that the students can attempt to tackle, especially when the teacher knows that the students have acquired the rules needed to solve the problem. Group investigation, role playing, synectics, simulation and nondirective teaching models can be used for developing problem solving.

TEACHING TASKS

Gagné emphasizes that *it is the learner's activity that results in the learning.* It is the teacher's responsibility to provide conditions that will increase the probability of student learning. Practice is extremely important so that the learner makes the necessary connections, but it is the learner who makes the connections, even when they are pointed out to him or her. *The teacher cannot substitute his or her own activity for that of the student.* We agree completely with Gagné on this point.

Teachers help students learn to use the different classes of learning by incorporating the following seven functions into their lessons and curriculum units:

1 informing the learner of the objectives;
2 presenting stimuli;
3 increasing learners' attention;
4 helping the learner recall what he or she has previously learned;
5 providing conditions that will evoke performance;
6 determining sequences of learning;
7 prompting and guiding the learning.

Also the teacher continuously encourages the student to generalize what he or she is learning so that the new skills and knowledge will be transformed into other situations.

Informing the learner of the performance expected is critical for providing him or her with a definite goal. For example, the teacher might say 'Today we're going to try to learn about three prime ministers. We'll learn their names, when they lived, and what they are most known for.' The teacher then presents the pictures of Benjamin Disraeli, Winston Churchill and Margaret Thatcher. Their names are printed under the pictures. Pointing to the pictures and names, and saying the names will draw the students' attention.

To recall previous learning, the teacher may say 'Do you remember that we discussed how our country has changed in various ways? Can you tell me what some of these changes were?' The students can reach into their memories and stimulate themselves with material that will later be connected to the prime ministers.

To induce performance, the teacher may ask the students to name the three prime ministers and then read printed material describing the life of each. Then the teacher can ask them to tell him or her what they have learned.

A variety of sequences can be used, depending on the type of learning and the subject matter in question. Generally, however, presenting a stimulus, evoking attention, helping the learner understand the objectives, inducing performance, and then helping the learner to generalize are major sequential teaching tasks that follow each other naturally.

Gagné's paradigm reminds us of a variety of important general principles of teaching: informing the learner of the levels of objectives being sought, encouraging generalization and pushing for application of what is learned.

Gagné emphasizes that we cannot control learning, but we can increase the probability that certain kinds of learning behaviour will occur. We can present stimuli in close connection and ask the student to perform, but it is the *student* who makes the connection between the printed and spoken word. Our careful design of lessons increases the probability of student learning and makes the learning process more sure, more predictable and more efficient. 'But, the individual nervous system [of each learner] must still make its own individual contribution. The nature of that contribution is, of course, what defines the need for the study of individual differences' (Gagné 1965: 291–313).

From this point of view, a model of teaching brings structures to the student that change the probability that he or she will learn certain things. The phases of the models present tasks to the student; the instructional moves of the teacher pull the student toward certain responses; and the social system generates a need for particular kinds of interaction with others. The net effect is to make it more likely that various kinds of

Table 11.1 Models especially appropriate for varieties of performance

Types of performance	Models of learning – tools for teaching				
Specific responding	Mnemonic	Simulations	Phase 1 inductive thinking	Phase 1 of concept attainment	Group investigation (data gathering activities)
Chaining	Mnemonic	Inductive thinking			
Multiple discrimination	Inductive thinking	Concept attainment			
Classifying	Inductive thinking	Concept attainment			
Rule using	Simulations	Concept attainment	Inductive thinking (application phase)		
Problem solving	Group investigation	Role playing	Synectics	Simulations	Nondirective

learning will take place. In Table 11.1, the models of learning and teaching shared in this book are paired with the six classes of learning/varieties of performance that Gagné has identified.

Gagné's hierarchy is useful in helping us select models appropriate for varieties of curriculum objectives. It also reminds us of the multiple types of learning promoted by individual models and the attention that must be given to the varieties of performance as the students engage in the study of any important topic. For example, students using inductive thinking to explore a problem in international relations, such as the balance of payments, will gather data (specific responding and chaining), organize it (multiple discrimination and classifying), and develop principles (rule using) to explore solutions to problems (problem solving).

PLANNING FOR TEACHING

Let's see what happens when we put Gagné's hierarchy to work. Let's design a global education curriculum that we can use from primary school all the way through secondary school. Such a complex curriculum will give us the opportunity to consider quite a range of models and, almost certainly, we will want to use several of them to design the instructional aspects of such a curriculum. We'll begin with a somewhat arbitrary statement of our overall objectives: to ensure that the students have a working knowledge of human geography, can think about some of the critical issues facing the peoples of the world and are prepared to interact productively with people from cultures other than theirs. Our rationale is that the global perspective is essential for personal understanding, for the guidance of our country, for the betterment of the world and for economic competence. At one level, we want our students to leave secondary school with the learning that will enable them to spin a globe, put a finger down on a land mass and know considerable information about the country it lights on. At another level, we want them to have considerable knowledge of several representative cultures and to be able to think of the world and our country in terms of cultural history and cultural comparison. At yet another level, we want them to have experience thinking about and generating solutions to important global problems.

A secondary overall objective is to use the study of the globe to further the English curriculum, especially the reading and writing of expository prose. Other objectives will appear as we think through our curriculum design and consider the classes of learning developed through the various models of teaching.

Now, let's think about the classes of learning and the teaching tasks that form part of our daily lessons and our longer curriculum units or schemes of work, and about the use of these in clarifying our curriculum objectives into content and skills and in selecting the most efficient model of teaching.

Specific responding. We want our students to recognize basic information about different countries: their names, where they are, and demographic information such as indicators of wealth (gross national product), indicators of population (size, fertility rates), of health (health care facilities, longevity) and culture (linguistic data, religious heritage, cultural groups). For this, we might use mnemonics and the inductive model, teaching the names of the countries and asking students to classify the countries with respect to basic demographic information.

Chaining. We might ask the students to collect information about the kind of life that is lived within these countries and to begin to develop pictures about how the demographic information might relate to quality of life. For this class of learning, we might continue to use mnemonics and the inductive model.

Multiple discrimination. We might ask the students to develop matrices that allow the countries to be classified on multiple variables, such as how types of government are related to the rights of women. For this class of learning, we might use both the inductive model and the concept attainment model.

Classifying. We might ask the students to develop typologies of countries and to generate maps that permit sets of variables to be used to generate pictures that lead to correlations, such as whether educational levels, industrial capacity, commercial activity and family structures are associated with one another. For this class of learning, we would surely use the inductive model of teaching.

Rule using. We might ask the students to create predictions about how the countries can be expected to respond to various types of conditions, such as population growth, ecological crises and natural disasters. For this class of learning, the application phases of concept attainment and the inductive model, and the simulation model, would be highly efficient.

Problem solving. We might present the students with sets of problems that can only be dealt with from an international perspective, such as cooperation to solve ecological problems and conflicts of various sorts (e.g. fishing rights, deforestation, nuclear testing, protection of the ozone layer). We might ask students to use the group investigation model to analyse the positions that underlie decisions about international cooperation. We might also ask them to categorize changes that are currently affecting the international situation (such as population growth and new trade agreements) and to predict the types of problems that are developing in the international community.

Using Gagné's framework along with models of teaching allows us to think about the knowledge and/or skills we want to teach, analyse them for the class of learning they require, then design our lessons to increase the probability that students will learn the curriculum content we have selected as most worthy.

We had written most of the text for this chapter before visiting Hempshill Hall school. During our visits, and with the theme of this chapter in mind, we used the Gagné framework as a means of reflecting

on our experiences in the school and of auditing the children's curricular experiences. Using Table 11.1 as the basis of our review we found
an impressive scatter of both performance type and range of learning
model. We were encouraged by this and recommend this as a review
technique for any school interested in 'models of learning – tools for
teaching'.

12 Teaching and learning together

A school teaches in three ways: by what it teaches, by how it teaches, and by the kind of place it is.

Lawrence Downey (1967)

Inquiry into teaching and learning makes the life of educators. We create environments, study how our students respond and watch them learn how to learn. Our position is that reflection on teaching can be greatly enhanced through the study of teaching strategies that have been submitted to intense scrutiny and development. Practice, theory and research become intertwined, and the body of professional knowledge becomes enhanced as each of us generates information about student learning.

In this chapter, we consider the processes by which teachers, working alone, can enhance their repertoires of teaching models, and how a whole school staff can do so. We also discuss the nature of inservice and school improvement initiatives which have been provided by local education authorities or school districts and external agencies to support individual practitioners and school staffs in this endeavour.

In all three instances, we have research to help us. Studies of teachers learning models of teaching indicate that there are three types of learning mingled together:

1 developing an understanding of the model, how it works, why it works, and how it can be modulated to take individual differences into account;
2 getting a picture of the model in action, envisioning what the teacher does and what the students do, and how the instructional and social environments are managed;
3 adapting the model to what one teaches – the goals of the parts of the curriculum for which one is responsible.

The first involves lots of reading and discussion – getting hold of the books and articles that describe the model and its rationale and analysing them thoroughly.

The second requires watching demonstrations and analysing them so that the process becomes clear. One begins to 'feel' the model in action and sense how to teach the students to use it as a tool for learning. Our rule of thumb is that one has to see a 'new' model about 20 times to get that feel.

The third is adaptation of the model to one's teaching situation – practising until executive control over the model is achieved. Forty or fifty hours of classroom practice are needed, plus the preparation time for that many hours of instruction.

Optimally, these three learning processes are mixed. One reads, watches, reads some more, watches and practises, reads and watches and practises, and so on . . .

WORKING AS AN INDIVIDUAL

Suppose that you (a head, teacher, adviser or academic) decide to study models of teaching and have no colleague willing to join you? (If there is someone available, then enlist that person immediately, for it will make the process much easier!) No matter, you can do it yourself. You just have to figure out how you can manage the three types of learning while working alone. Here are some of our 'tested' suggestions:

1 *Study* just one model at a time and keep at it until you have mastered it.
2 *Read* anything you can get your hands on pertinent to the model. *Models of Teaching* (Joyce and Weil 1996) is a handy guide to the literature.
3 See if you can find a workshop conducted by someone who is an expert in using the model. Make sure the workshop includes lots of *demonstrations*. If you can't find a workshop, then obtain videotapes of the model in action and study them (a few tapes, watched again and again, help a lot).
4 *Practise* like crazy. Prepare short lessons and long units (both are necessary). After a few practices with your students, read some more and watch the tapes again and then practise. Make sure your practice is regular – don't let long periods go by between them – and that the practice is within your normal content area, where you have the greatest substantive control. You will feel uncomfortable at first. Ignore the discomfort and keep practising. After a few tries, you will begin to get the feel of the moves of the model, and the adaptation to your curriculum area, or schemes of work, will become easier.

Be sure to study what the students are learning, both substance and how to learn.

WORKING AS A WHOLE SCHOOL STAFF

Suppose you are working with a staff that is studying teaching strategies. How would you proceed, based on what we currently 'know' about school improvement and student achievement?

1 Organize peer coaching or partnership teaching groups. First, form partners from within the staff – one or two people, no more – who can work together to study the new teaching strategy or strategies. Develop a weekly schedule for peer coaching, or partnership teaching, close to an hour each week, when the partners can meet, preferably in the same setting at the same time, to share plans and progress.

2 The staff needs to study one model at a time, arrangements to do just one are difficult enough.

3 The rest of the process is the same as if you were working alone: studying the literature of the model, watching demonstrations and practising, except that you now have the companionship of others as you work toward effective implementation.

Working in this way allows you to exploit some dimensions of a model more rapidly and powerfully, as is seen in the following two examples. The first demonstrates how teachers can have a cumulative impact on pupils throughout the school when all pupils are taught a model of learning. In the second we see how an entire staff studies the effects of a specific model of teaching on student achievement.

In one English secondary school in which we have been working a decision was taken to establish teachers' use of *cooperative group work* as a priority for school improvement. Progress was smooth during the early stages, as each curriculum department scrutinized its own practice and identified instances where groups were used as a deliberate teaching strategy. However, when the staff came together to share their experience, it quickly became apparent that the various departments, and even individual teachers within departments, construed group work very differently. A planned inservice day became a frustrating experience, as the more the teachers struggled to create a dialogue about their own and colleagues' practice, the clearer it became that they were talking about different things.

Fortunately the commitment of the teachers involved to move forward did not prevent them from seeing the need to go backwards first. Over the following weeks they systematically explored the range of possible activities which were frequently, and rather loosely, referred to as *group work*. Deliberate efforts were made to review relevant literature and research and to sort out a basic typology which would allow the teachers to locate their own strategies and to compare similarities and differences. Out of this emerged agreed definitions which were common to all the staff group, who now had a greatly increased level of common understanding and a shared vocabulary. This enabled not only much more meaningful discourse during partnership teaching, but it also meant that students throughout the school were exposed to a consistent model of learning.

In the second example the teachers of Kaiser Elementary School in the Newport/Costa Mesa School District have been learning to use the inductive model of teaching to help their pupils connect reading and writing. The objective is to see if the children can generate better quality writing by analysing how expert writers work. For example, when studying how to introduce characters, the children classify the approaches used by authors in the books they are reading. They then experiment with the literary devices they have identified.

Periodically the teachers ask the children to produce writing elicited with standardized content and prompts. For example, the children watch a segment of film that introduces a character and then are asked to provide a written introduction to the character. These samples of writing are scored with an instrument that has been developed at the UCLA Center for Research on Evaluation (Quellmatz and Burry 1983) to measure quality of writing across the grades, and which yields scores on three dimensions of quality.

The year before the teachers began to study the teaching of writing with the inductive model, the average child's gain in writing quality during a year was about 20 points on the scale. For example, the grade 4 average climbed from a score of 180 to a score of 200. The grade 6 average moved from about 220 to about 240. As the teachers taught the children to make the connection between reading and writing, the average gain for a year jumped to about 90 points. The average child gained about four and a half times more than the average gain the previous year. No child gained less than 40 points. Some gained as much as 140 points.

The Kaiser teachers surveyed the research on the teaching of writing and found some examples of what looked like large gains when particular curriculum approaches were implemented. They wondered how they could compare the results of their efforts when some of the studies used different scales.

When the Kaiser School staff discovered the concept of effect size (see Appendix 1), they were able to calculate the effects of their efforts in such a way that they could compare their results to those of other efforts. They consulted the review of research on writing conducted by George Hillocks and found that the average effect size of 'inquiry' approaches to the teaching of writing was 0.67 compared to textbook-orientated instruction. The average student in the average treatment was at about the 70th percentile of the distributions of students taught by the textbook method.

For each grade the Kaiser teachers carefully calculated the effect size. For example, their sixth grade had gained an average of 90 points compared with an average of 20 the previous year (the control), a difference of 70 points. The standard deviation of the control year was 55. Dividing 55 into 70 they calculated an effect size of 1.27, nearly twice the average in the Hillocks review. The average student in the first year of the use of the inductive model was at approximately the 90th percentile of the distribution of the control year.

The teachers in both these schools are inquirers. They conduct individual and school-wide action research. They selected a model of teaching, studied it, learned how to use it and inquired into its effects on their students. Their collective inquiry and its results on student learning will lead them to search for ways of using that model across curriculum areas and to look for and create other models that can serve their students. They are classic 'teacher researchers'.

FOR A TEACHER INSERVICE CENTRE, EXTERNAL SUPPORT AGENCY OR SCHOOL IMPROVEMENT NETWORK

Now, suppose that you are responsible for the organization of a teacher inservice centre sponsored by a local education authority or school improvement initiative organized by a university. Part of your job is to support school-based school improvement and to help teachers study, generate and use alternative models of teaching.

Just as in the individual and staff examples, you will need to provide the conditions that permit people to learn. As we have already seen, this involves the study of the literature, study of demonstrations, and practice with support, preferably by peer coaching teams; thus your workshops need to contain the elements that support those conditions.

Your offerings can be to individuals, groups (better), entire staff (even better) or the staff of an entire consortium of schools (can work very well).

Participants need to be organized into peer coaching teams or part-nerships, with time provided for them to meet and study together. Participants will need help learning how to study student learning in an action research framework. Participants will need to study implementation of the model and its effects on students so that they can assess the results of their efforts.

Here is an example of a teaching centre effort, done by the organizers of the Richmond County, Georgia, School Improvement Program. The intention from the beginning of the Richmond Program was to increase the capacity of the school district as a unit to sustain and expand school improvement initiatives, thus reducing and then eliminating the need for external support. A primary means for increasing local capacity was the development of a community of teachers and heads who could carry forward all phases of the initiative, introducing more schools to the processes outlined above, providing the staff development on models of teaching, supporting study groups and building leadership teams, and giving help to other groups of schools.

The cadre was recruited from the pool of teachers who had made out-standing progress with models of teaching and who showed leadership in their schools in study groups and in supporting school-wide efforts. Those wishing to be candidates for the cadre submitted videotapes of their use of each model in the classroom. The selection team visited those persons in their classrooms, watched them teach and interviewed them.

An initial cadre group of 20 persons was organized to receive additional training beyond that provided to the other teachers and heads.

The additional training included how to organize staff and study groups and how to conduct training and study implementation.

The Richmond cadre of teachers disseminated the teaching strategies to other schools in the district. Results for the first nine schools on the state-wide standardized tests were substantial. Each of the nine schools completed eight tests for a total of 72 test scores. Forty of the 72 scores reflected gains of greater than four months over the previous year's results, and twenty of the 72 scores reflected gains of between two and four months.

In Britain, examples of such initiatives are found in the case ex-amples emanating from the 'Improving the Quality of Education for All' school improvement project (Hopkins *et al.* 1994, 1996). During times of great educational change, the central concern of the IQEA project has been to raise student achievement through focusing on the teaching/learning process and the conditions which support it. The project works from an assumption that schools are most likely to strengthen their ability to provide enhanced outcomes for all pupils when they adopt ways of working that are consistent both with their own aspirations as a school community and the national reform agenda. Indeed to an extent, these schools are using the impetus of external reform for internal purpose as they navigate the systemic changes of recent years.

At the outset of IQEA, a set of principles were outlined that provided a philosophical and practical starting point. These principles embodied a set of core values about school improvement of which two are key:

- school improvement is a process that focuses on enhancing the *quality of students' learning*;
- the school will seek to develop structures and create conditions which encourage collaboration and lead to the *empowerment* of individuals and groups.

Experience suggests that these principles create synergy around change as they inform the thinking and actions of teachers during school improvement efforts. These principles also underpin one of the central characteristics of successful school improvement, which is that *teachers talk to each other about teaching*. School improvement strategies should therefore help teachers create a discourse about, and language for, teaching. On the basis of the IQEA experience, this is best achieved through:

- teachers discussing with each other the nature of teaching strategies and their application to classroom practice and schemes of work;
- establishing specifications or guidelines for the chosen teaching strategies;
- agreeing on standards used to assess student progress as a result of employing a range of teaching methods;
- mutual observation and partnership teaching in the classroom.

REFLECTION

Studying teaching pays off! A knowledge base exists that can help individuals, staffs and entire regions expand the repertoire of teaching/learning opportunities available to students. All it takes to get started is the willingness to inquire into this knowledge base, to inquire into our teaching practice, and to inquire more fully into what and how students learn.

Coda: educational policy and the study of teaching

Few teachers see themselves as policymakers. Frequently, in fact, teachers pass part of the time of day in vocal dissent with the attempts of national and local policymakers to change or improve the quality of education. Be that as it may, many contemporary strategies for school improvement place teachers in the role of policymakers or, more frequently, in roles as co-policymakers with those who work at the national or local levels. The more teachers are brought into the process of how education is conducted and improved, the more important it is that issues about the role of education in society be brought into the regular dialogue about teaching.

Thus we conclude this little book on the study of learning and teaching with a memorandum to those whose work at any level makes them responsible for thinking about where society is going and how education should travel with it. We are particularly concerned to emphasize the relationship between the study of teaching and initiatives of any type to increase the effectiveness of schools. Much of the substance of the memorandum deals with the assumptions and initiatives that are characteristic of the governmental level of policymaker. Mildly transformed, we also hope their relevance to school-based efforts will be apparent.

THE OLD SCHOOLHOUSE AND THE POST-WORLD WAR II SOCIETY

In the course of the last half of the twentieth century, the industrialized nations have changed in a number of ways that have affected the relationship between education and the nature of society. This has raised expectations for performance and expanded the range of areas where schools are relied on to solve problems. Consequently public attention is frequently focused on whether schools have kept pace with society's rising and widening expectations; questions are continually raised about whether the common school, created as it was in the nineteenth century, meets the demands of the emerging world. And many people feel that it doesn't.

The curriculum and processes of that nineteenth-century common school assumed that it was important for all citizens to have at least primitive skills in reading and writing. Advanced preparation for the professions and the conduct of research and cultural innovation would, however, be the province of a few students privileged by their own ability or socioeconomic advantage.

Since World War II it has been increasingly recognized that education must generate a much higher level of literacy for all, including those who receive the most advanced training. It is also imperative that schools provide the skills for lifelong learning and the skills of inquiry which are far more complex than the primitive reading/writing skills that were seen as an adequate product of basic education 150 years ago.

In addition, society doesn't know where else to turn to solve several serious problems. Among them, a culture of poverty threatens the quality of urban life, and its millions of direct victims have to be supported by the more fortunate. The threat of crime has become real to everyone. Effective schools are certainly a more desirable alternative to expanding prisons and devoting more resources to detection and incarceration.

Immigration is an example of a change-producing phenomenon that generates special problems – the swift learning of new languages and employable skills – that can only be solved by rapid adaptation by schools, as nations may have to assimilate several million new citizens within the space of a decade. In the past, societies normally allowed newcomers several generations to assimilate into the economic mainstream and, in the meantime, a strong back and a willingness to do anything for a living would provide them with at least a survival-level income. Assimilation now must be rapid, for 'entry-level' jobs have diminished and, even where they exist, will no longer provide adequate incomes.

Thus in an astonishingly short span of time the role of education in the lives of citizens has changed dramatically. A few decades ago a little formal education could provide the knowledge and skill to participate fully and satisfyingly in society, albeit for some at a disadvantage with respect to their highly educated neighbours. Now, post-secondary training is an essential for today's entry-level jobs, and continuing adult education, including self-education, is vital as the nature of work evolves and requires life-long retooling.

The ponderous methods of our familiar old schools are suddenly thrust into a world where their inefficiencies are intolerable.

The teachers in those schools came into a system where change was glacially slow and the methods of the past were handed down to them in comfortable confidence that they would suffice for a few more decades. Pre-service training was meagre and built around a brief apprenticeship designed to transmit normative teaching styles which were largely unquestioned. Continuing education for teachers was not thought necessary; the old school simply did not have a staff development system. Teachers worked in relative isolation. Neither time for collegial interchange nor a process for collective study and action was provided in their workplace. Briefly trained, isolated from one another, unsupported by continuing education for themselves, teachers tried to make the improvements they could.

The heightened awareness of the critical importance of quality education has generated pressure on government policymakers to strengthen the school and change it. Initiatives to do so are now a familiar part of the educational landscape.

SOME EARLY INITIATIVES AND MISTAKES

In the immediate postwar period government initiatives responded positively to a rising school-age population and a demand by demobilized soldiers for post-secondary opportunities. The focus however was on making additions to the old schoolhouse, not on changing what went on inside it.

Government efforts based on dissatisfaction with the quality of curriculum and instruction started in the late 1950s. The huge scale of the social changes that were taking place had not yet been fully understood – the 1950s/60s movement was directed at modernizing what was taught and how it was taught. Examples include the efforts in the UK based on the Plowden Report (Central Advisory Council for Education (England) 1967), and the 'Academic Reform Movement' (Bruner 1961; Joyce and Weil 1996) in the United States. These, as did most of the other interventions of the time, challenged the content and process of schooling as antiquated. Some very interesting approaches to curriculum and teaching were developed and researched. *However, the weakness of pre-service education combined with the lack of a staff development system to provide adequate implementation meant that they disappeared from most schools within a few years* (Goodlad and Klein 1970; Sarason 1982). The courses and workshops designed to carry these reforms were simply too few and too weak. In both countries efforts by government to influence education fell by the wayside for lack of the ability to help teachers learn how to use them.

General curricular and instructional reform was not attempted on a large scale in the 1970s and 1980s, but two components were added to the system: a large-scale effort to expand services to children who have learning disabilities but who are not profoundly handicapped; and the other to increase attention to the children of the poor. The weakness of the systems for preparing pre-service or inservice teachers has unfortunately largely defeated these initiatives (Joyce and Showers 1995), as it has the smaller programmes designed to teach English to those for whom it is a second language. Academic achievement in schools is about the same as it was before those programmes were expanded. We are fairly sure that the primary reason for this is that curricula and teaching

strategies that can make a difference to those populations are not implemented because inservice programmes for teachers are inadequate.

RECENT GOVERNMENT EFFORTS

During the last ten years there has been a coalescence of opinion that
schools need to become more effective, that innovations in curricula
and teaching methods are now urgent, and that generally something
must be done. A considerable variety of initiatives have been generated
by governments. The variety is derived from the quite different, sometimes almost opposite, assumptions on which it is based. These are both
about the direction of change and the ways in which government can
be effective in instigating reform.

Because the stakes are so high, both direction and method need close
examination, especially because government efforts have had such a
poor history.

Improvement through accountability. A cluster of related assumptions
about accountability for performance underlies a good many proposals.
The core assumption holds that enunciating higher standards and
making schools accountable for meeting those standards through pub-
licity about test performance (i.e. league tables) will force schools to
generate initiatives to improve themselves. A closely related assumption
is that allowing parents actively to choose the schools their children will
attend will provide some high octane motivation to improve.

The accountability-based approach has considerable support from
'private sector' thinking. It is a culturally comfortable assumption, for
most people believe that businesses survive and private sector personnel are evaluated on the basis of measures of performance. Thus
accountability-driven reform feels intuitively correct to most people,
yet the idea is radical to most *school* people.

We believe, however, that the idea rests on a commonly tacit
assumption that is erroneous. It is the teachers who have a reservoir of
energy and a curricular and instructional knowledge and skill that they
are not using, but which will burst forth under pressure. We believe that
teachers are currently doing the best they can with what they know and
that modernization will depend on very large-scale staff development
so that teachers can learn and develop the content and methods necessary for our times. Providing pressure without the opportunity for study
and training will simply not work. The private sector knows this well in
the context of running businesses. No successful business would expect
a change of procedure without providing training.

The accountability-orientated procedures have been embedded in
educational organizations for some time – 'league tables' and 'test
scores' are published in local papers, and newsletters containing comparisons are sent to parents and communities, all without effect.

Advocates would do well to examine that evidence before they
proceed further and, in future initiatives, to include the resources to

develop the staff development system that will be necessary if teachers are to develop fresh knowledge and skills.

Decentralization: improvement through 'site-based' or 'local' control. There is a widely held negative assumption that excessive regulation by educational bureaucrats and excessive control by local governors has held down the energy and creativity of schools. Equally widespread is a movement to make each individual school responsible for creating a modern and outstanding education.

Decentralization is an offshoot of a movement in private sector organizational development that believes worker involvement in assessing productivity and worker-generated initiatives to be essential in any efforts to modernize the system (as Deming so graphically illustrated). Some but not all advocates believe that the demands on specific schools are so unique that local control is the only practical way to govern them.

The flaw in this approach is the same tacit assumption that undermines the accountability orientation: that schools can regenerate themselves without either the support of an extensive staff development system or the time to study and make school-wide initiatives in curriculum and teaching. It is unrealistic to assume that the staff of schools – currently operating virtually without common time for study and planning – can renew themselves or turn into self-renewing organizations by simply removing bureaucratic controls.

Removing regulations will not automatically generate creativity. The poor productivity of the 'site-based' initiatives in the United States, and to some extent 'opting out' in England, is evidence and needs to be taken very seriously. Again, the application of what has come to be called 'total quality management' in the private sector did not ignore provision for training, yet time for reflective inquiry is generally overlooked in education.

Returning to the halcyon days of yore. Some proposals for reform, including some of the accountability-through-testing ones, are based on the assumption that the traditional educational system was really quite good, but that we drifted away from it, and the system would work fine again if there was a return to the curriculum and methods of 100 years ago. When this assumption prevails, the tests that are chosen focus on basic but primitive literacy skills and ignore the more complex cognitive skills and structures of knowledge. Partly the belief that we need to return to the basics has been brought about by a concerted 'media blitz' by educational arch-conservatives, who may be actually nostalgic for a society where educational privileges are doled out on a selective basis. This brand of conservatism does not envision an educational system that confers opportunity on all people – it is built around the perpetuation of an educational system that leaves many students unable to read and write effectively, creates phobias about the learning of mathematics, science and foreign languages, and has a few other obnoxious side-effects. However, certain organizations have been effective in creating a myth that the 'good old education' has disappeared, even when it has not and when in fact it can't do the job demanded by today's world.

Similarly, some proposals are based on the assumption that educational reforms have been responsible for a weakening of the educational system and that the traditional 'basic system' was inherently sound and should not be changed. To some extent this assumption arises from the desire of parents (nearly all of us) that the education of our children be familiar and completely intelligible to us. A different system for curriculum and teaching – that offers our children opportunities we did not have – creates a 'generational jealousy' of sorts. In a subliminal way, we wonder what would happen if we spawned a generation of wonderful poets and playwrights, tremendous scholars and integrative politicians. To modernize education we have to accept the fact that we all have to catch up with the times and embrace the construction of an education that will confer on our children opportunities we never had.

INVESTING IN PEOPLE AND DEVELOPMENT

The core of educational modernization will depend on the development of a completely different workplace for teachers, one where teaching and curriculum are studied continuously, student learning is studied intensively, and the whole staff work cohesively to make initiatives to improve the school. All initiatives will founder, though, unless the workplace is changed radically so that time is built in to every week for study and development – not just preparation by individuals for specific lessons – but for collective mastery of new teaching strategies and the development of new curriculum plans.

The powerful existing base of knowledge about curriculum and teaching needs to be made available to teachers for their immediate use as they invent new ways of creating powerful learning experiences for their students. In addition, resources need to be made available for research and development on teaching and learning so that the knowledge base becomes larger and better. School/university partnerships can easily be developed in the interest of research.

We urge policymakers to instigate a kind of restructuring that creates time for collegial study and decision making and ensures that what has been called 'staff development' becomes a regular and ongoing feature of every school. There is a burgeoning knowledge base about school improvement, and the list of documented successful projects is growing (for example Hopkins et al. 1996; Joyce and Calhoun 1996; Slavin 1996; Hopkins, in press). As far as we can tell, the collegial study of teaching has been at the core of every documented successful initiative.

That all this is possible is shown through the scenarios provided in this book. We have cited examples from all over the world to demonstrate that powerful learning does not occur by accident, and that powerful teaching is not serendipitous. To illustrate how the workplace can be adapted to support both powerful learning and powerful teaching we have also provided an extended case study, and a continuing series of reflections on this theme, from one of our favourite schools – Hempshill Hall school, Nottingham. If schools such as this can, in less than auspicious circumstances, provide such quality learning environments for their pupils, why can't others?

While we ponder the educational policy/student achievement conundrum, Ron Edmonds' evocative question returns to haunt us: 'How many effective schools would you have to see to be persuaded of the educability of all children?' Edmonds answered his own question like this: 'We already know more than we need to do that. Whether or not we do it, must depend on how we feel about the fact that we haven't so far' (Edmonds 1979: 22–3).

Schooling can be improved dramatically, but only if the workplace includes a far more precise study of student progress than is now the case, and if teachers work continuously on their skills. We believe that every initiative made at governmental level needs to be accompanied by a clear and practical commitment to increase the capability of the schools to inquire into educational practice and to improve it. This implies that teachers in their turn create the conditions for powerful learning – where the models of learning described in this book do in reality become tools for teaching.

The concept of effect size

We use the concept of 'effect size' (Glass 1982) to describe the magnitude of gains from any given change in educational practice and thus to predict what we can hope to accomplish by using that practice.

To introduce the idea, let us consider a study conducted by Dr Bharati Baveja (1988) with one of the authors in the Motilal Nehru School of Sports about 30 miles north-west of New Delhi, India. Dr Baveja designed her study to test the effectiveness of an inductive approach to a botany unit compared with an intensive tutorial treatment. All of the students were given a test at the beginning of the unit to assess their knowledge before instruction began and were divided into two groups equated on the basis of achievement. The control group studied the material with the aid of tutoring and lectures on the material – the standard treatment in Indian schools for courses of this type. The experimental group worked in pairs and were led through inductive and concept attainment exercises emphasizing classification of plants.

Figure A1.1 shows the distribution of scores for the experimental and control groups on the post-test which, like the pre-test, contained items dealing with the information pertaining to the unit.

The difference between the experimental and control groups was a little above a standard deviation. The difference, computed in terms of standard deviations, is the *effect size of the inductive treatment*. What that means is that the experimental group average score was where the 80th percentile score was for the control group. The difference increased when a delayed recall test was given ten months later, indicating that the information acquired with the concept-orientated strategies was retained somewhat better than information gained via the control treatment.

Calculations like these enable us to compare the magnitude of the potential effects of the innovations (teaching skills and strategies,

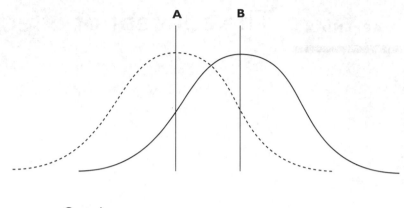

-------- Control group
———— Experimental group
A = Control group mean
B = Experimental group mean

Figure A1.1 Compared distributions for experimental and control groups (from Baveja 1988)

curricula and technologies) that we might use in an effort to affect student learning. We can also determine whether the treatment has different effects for all kinds of students or just for some. In the Baveja (1988) study the experimental treatment was apparently effective for the whole population. The lowest score in the experimental group distribution was about where the 30th percentile score was for the control group; about 30 per cent of the students exceeded the highest score obtained in the control.

Although substantial in its own right, learning and retention of information was modest when we consider the effect on the students' ability to identify plants and their characteristics, which was measured on a separate test. The scores by students from the experimental group were *eight* times higher than the scores for the control group. Dr Baveja's inquiry confirmed her hypothesis that the students, using the inductive model, were able to apply the information and concepts from the unit much more effectively than were the students from the tutorial treatment.

FURTHER INQUIRY INTO EFFECT SIZE

Let's work through some concepts that are useful in describing distributions of scores to deepen our understanding a bit.

We describe distributions of scores in terms of the *central tendencies*, which refer to the clustering of scores around the middle of the distribution, and *variance*, or their dispersion. Concepts describing central tendency include the *average* or arithmetic mean, which is computed by summing the scores and dividing by the number of scores, and the median or middle score (half of the others are above and half below

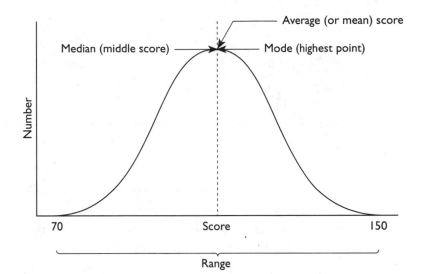

Figure A1.2 A sample normal distribution

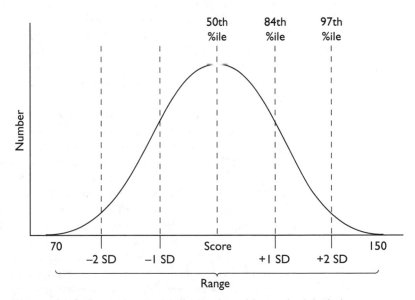

Figure A1.3 A sample normal distribution with standard deviations

the median score), and the *mode*, which is the most frequent score (graphically, the highest point in the distribution). In Figure A1.2 the median, the average and the mode are all in the same place, because the distribution is completely symmetrical.

Dispersion is described in terms of the *range* (the distance between the highest and lowest scores), the rank, which is frequently described as the *percentile* (the twentieth score from the top in a 100-person distribution is at the 80th percentile because 20 per cent of the scores are above

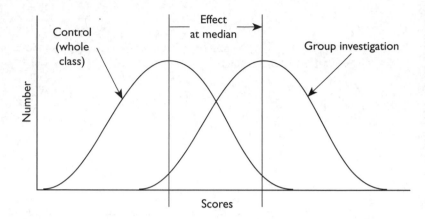

Figure A1.4 A sample depiction of effect size (from Sharan and Shachar 1988)

and 80 per cent are below it), and the *standard deviation*, which describes how widely or narrowly scores are distributed. In Figure A1.3 the range is from 70 (the lowest score) to 150 (the highest score). The 50th percentile score is at the middle (in this case corresponding with the average, the mode and the median). The standard deviations are marked off by the vertical lines labelled +1 SD, +2 SD, and so on. Note that the percentile rank of the score one standard deviation above the mean is 84 (84 per cent of the scores are below that point); the rank two standard deviations above the mean is 97; and three standard deviations above the mean is 99.

When the mean, median and mode coincide as in these distributions, and the distribution of scores is as symmetrical as the ones depicted in these figures, the distribution is referred to as *normal*. This concept is very useful in statistical operations, although many actual distributions are not symmetrical, as we will see.

However, to explain the concept of effect size, we will use symmetrical, 'normal' distributions before illustrating how the concept works with differently shaped distributions. Figure A1.4 compares the post-test scores of the low SES students in chapter 7 between the 'whole class' and 'group investigation' treatments. The average score of the 'group investigation' treatment corresponds to about the 92nd percentile of the distribution of the 'whole class' students. The effect size is computed by dividing the difference between the two means by the standard deviation of the 'control' or 'whole class' group. The effect size in this case is 1.6 standard deviations using the formula:

$$\text{ES} = \text{average of experimental group} - \frac{\text{average of control}}{\text{standard deviation of control}}$$

Figures like these provide an idea about the relative effects one can expect if one teaches students with each model of teaching compared with using the normative patterns of curriculum and instruction. We create each figure from an analysis of the research base that is currently

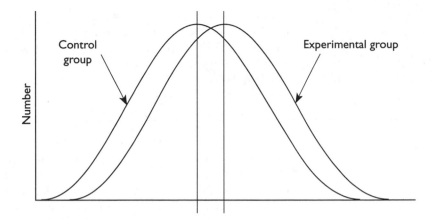

Figure A1.5 A sample effect size: ability scores (from Spaulding 1970)

available and will usually build the figure to depict the average effects from large numbers of studies.

When using the research base to decide when to use a given model of teaching it is important to realize that size of effects is not the only consideration. We have to consider the nature of the objectives and the uses of the model. For example, in Spaulding's (1970) study, the effect size on ability measures was just 0.5, or about a half standard deviation (see Figure A1.5).

However, ability is a very powerful attribute, and a model or combination of models that can increase ability will have an effect on everything the student does for years to come, by increasing learning through those years. The simplest cooperative learning procedures have relatively modest effect sizes, affecting feelings about self as a learner, social skills and academic learning, *and they are easy to use and have wide applications*. Thus their modest effect can be felt more regularly and broadly than some models that have more dramatic effect sizes with respect to a given objective.

Some models can help us virtually eliminate dispersion in a distribution. For example, a colleague of ours used mnemonic devices to teach his fourth grade students the names of the states and their capitals. *All* his students learned *all* of them and remembered them throughout the year. Thus the distribution of his class's scores on tests of their ability to supply all the names on a blank map had no range at all. The average score was the top possible score. There were no percentile ranks because the students' scores were all tied at the top. For some objectives – a basic reading vocabulary and computation skills, for example – we want, in fact, to have a very high degree of success for all our students because anything less is terribly disadvantaging for them – and for their society.

Although high effect sizes make a treatment attractive, size alone is not the only consideration when choosing among alternatives. Modest effect sizes that affect many persons can have a large payoff for the population. A comparison with medicine is worthwhile. Suppose a dread disease is affecting a population and we possess a vaccine that will reduce the chances of contracting the disease by only 10 per cent. If a million persons might become infected without the vaccine but 900,000 if it is used, the modest effect of the vaccine might save 100,000 lives. In education, some estimates suggest that during the first year of school in the USA about one million children each year (about 30 per cent) make little progress toward learning to read. We also know that lack of success in reading instruction is in fact a dread educational disease, since for each year that initial instruction is unsuccessful the probability that the student will respond to instruction later is greatly lowered. Would a modestly effective treatment, say one that reduced the lack of success in the first year for 50,000 children (5 per cent) be worthwhile? We think so. Also several such treatments might be cumulative. Of course we prefer a high effect treatment, but one is not always available. Even when it is, it might not reach some students and we might need to resort to a less powerful choice for those students.

Also there are different types of effects that need to be considered. Attitudes, values, concepts, intellectual development, skills and information are just a few. Keeping to the example of early reading, two treatments might be approximately equal in terms of learning to read in the short run, but one might affect attitudes positively and leave the students feeling confident and ready to try again. Similarly, two social studies programmes might achieve similar amounts of information and concepts, but one might excel in attitudes toward citizenship.

In the most dramatic instances, when the effect size reaches five or six standard deviations, the lowest scoring student in the experimental treatment exceeds the highest scoring student in the control treatment! This is a rare event, of course, but when it does occur, it gives us great hope about the potential of educational practice.

Again, as we describe some practices and the effects that can be expected from them, we should not concentrate on magnitude of effects alone. Self-instructional programmes that are no more effective than traditional teaching can be very useful because they enable students to learn by themselves. Broadcast television, because of its potential to reach so many children, can make a big difference even though it is modestly effective in comparison with standard instruction. *Sesame Street* is a well known example (Ball and Bogatz 1970). It is not dramatically more effective than early reading instruction that does not include it, but *Sesame Street* produces positive attitudes and augments the teaching of reading handsomely, enabling a certain percentage of students virtually to teach themselves. In fact, distance education and media-based instruction (learning from television, computer-assisted instruction and packages of multimedia materials) need not be more effective to be very useful. For example, in a secondary school that does not offer a given foreign language, a student who can learn that language by self-study assisted by television, computer programs and similar packages can be greatly benefited. The Open University, that operates as a distance education agency augmented by tutorial centres, has virtually doubled the number of university graduates in the UK. The performance of its students on academic tests compares favourably with the performance of 'regular' university students.

Some procedures can interact productively with others. One-to-one tutoring has a very large effect size (Bloom 1984) and might interact productively with some teaching strategies. Or, as is evidently the case within the 'Success for All' (Slavin *et al.* 1990; Slavin 1991) and 'Reading Recovery' (Pinnell 1989) programmes, it is incorporated within a curriculum management system that enables short periods of tutoring to pay off wonderfully. On the other hand, 'tracking' or 'streaming' hurts the effectiveness of any procedure (Oakes 1986).

Simply learning the size of effects of a year's instruction can be very informative, as we learned from the National Assessment of Writing Progress (Applebee *et al.* 1990), which discovered that the effect size of instruction in writing nationally is such that the average eighth grade student is about at the 62nd percentile of the fourth grade distribution! Schools may want to learn how much better they can do than that!

Measures of learning can be of many kinds. School grades are of great importance, as are measures of conduct such as counts of referrals and suspensions. In fact, staff development programmes want to give close attention to those measures as well as simple measures, such as how many books students read. Content analyses of student work are very important, as in the study of quality of writing. Curriculum-relevant tests (those that measure the content of a unit or course) are important. Finally, the traditional standardized tests can be submitted to an analysis that produces estimates of effect size.

Educational research is in its infancy. The state of the art is not such that any specific curricular or instructional models can solve *all* the problems of student learning. We hope that the readers of this book will not just use it as a source of teaching and learning strategies, but will learn how to add to the knowledge base. There are millions of teachers at work today. If only 1 per cent conducted and reported one study each year, there would be tens of thousands of new studies every year, a knowledge increment many times larger than the entire current research base. But aside from contributing to the larger knowledge base, teachers in any school can, by studying their teaching, share ideas that can help everyone in the school to become more effective.

Peer coaching guides

The following pages contain peer coaching guides for all the models of teaching contained in this book. These forms facilitate planning and communication between teachers who observe one another and try to profit from the observational experience. The forms can also be used to facilitate sharing of ideas by teachers, whether or not observation of one another's teaching is included.

Hence they are addressed to both parties in the peer coaching process: the teacher who is planning and directing the teaching episode and the partner who is studying the model. Both parties are involved in a continuing experiment on teaching. Each has the same purpose, which is to increase their ability to analyse the transactions between teacher and student, and their ability to teach students how to learn information and concepts. The guide is used both to assist the planning of the teaching episode and in focusing the observation on key features of the model. The teacher prepares the observer by filling out the entries where indicated. The observer fills in the observation checklist and communicates the result to the teacher. Both parties will profit most by making a partnership that studies the student responses and plans how to help the students learn more effectively. The observer is not present to advise the teacher on how to teach better but, rather, to learn by observing and help the teacher by providing information about the students' responses.

The communication of the analysis should be conducted in a neutral tone, proceeding matter-of-factly through the phases of the model. The guide draws attention to the syntax of the model – the cognitive and social tasks that are presented to the students and how the students respond, and the principles of reaction – the guidelines for reacting to the students as they try to attain the concept. The teacher may want to direct the coaching partner to look closely at a specific phase of the model, such as student response to a particular cognitive or social task, or reactions to student responses. The coaching partner should avoid giving gratuitous advice. Normally the communication about a teaching episode should be completed in five minutes or less. For self-coaching, teachers should use videotape when possible and, during playback, enter the role of partner, analysing the transactions as dispassionately as possible.

Learning to think inductively

The guide is designed to assist peer coaching of the inductive thinking model of learning and teaching. When planning questions, skip through the guide to the entries marked 'Teacher' and fill them in as needed. They will guide you through the model. Observers can use the guide to familiarize themselves with the plans of the teacher and to make notes about what is observed. Please remember, observers, that your primary function is not to give 'expert advice' to your colleague, but to observe the students as requested by the teacher and to observe the whole process so that you can gain ideas for your own teaching. The teacher is the coach in the sense that he or she is demonstrating a teaching episode for you. When you teach and are observed, you become the coach.

Teacher: do you want to suggest a focus for the analysis? If so, what is it?

_____

_____

THE TEACHING PROCESS

Most lessons have both content and process objectives. Content objectives identify subject matter (facts, concepts, generalizations, relationships) to be mastered by students, while process objectives specify skills and procedures students need in order to achieve content objectives or auxiliary social objectives (for example, cooperation in a learning task).

The content objectives for inductive thinking reside in the information and concepts embedded in a data set. Students categorize items in the data set by attributes held in common by subsets of items. For example, if the data set consisted of a collection of plants, students might classify plants by types of leaves (size, texture, pattern of veins, shape, connection of leaves to stems, etc.). Content objectives for this data set might include both information about specific plants and the building of a typology. Process objectives might include learning the scientific skill of the discipline (observation and classification) as well as the social skills of cooperative problem solving.

Content objective(s)

Teacher: what do you want students to gain from this classification task? What, in your opinion, are the critical attributes of the data set? What categories do you bring to the set?

_____

_____

Process objective(s)

Teacher: are the students familiar with the model? Do they need special assistance or training with respect to any aspect of the process? (For example, do students understand how to group items by common attributes? Can they work cooperatively with partners on a classification task?)

PHASE I: DATA COLLECTION/PRESENTATION

The primary activity of phase 1 of the inductive thinking model involves collecting or presentation of a data set. The teacher may provide a data set or instruct students to collect the data that will be categorized. The data that will be scrutinized by the students are extremely important, for they represent much of the information the students will learn from the episode. The choice between data collection or presentation is also important. To continue the above example, if students collect leaves, a different set of data will result than if they had been presented with them. Once a data set has been collected by or presented to students, the teacher may want to set parameters for the classification activity by orientating students to relevant attributes. For example, if the data are plants, the teacher may wish to narrow the field of observation by having students classify by types of leaves. On the other hand, the teacher may wish to leave the parameters open and simply instruct students to classify by common attributes. Generally speaking, the more open-ended the instructions, the better the results.

Items from a data set may be included in only one category or in multiple categories. You may want to experiment with different instructions regarding the classification of data and observe differences in the categories that result. Generally speaking, leaving open the possibility of multiple category membership for items from the data set provides the most energy.

Teacher: please describe the data set to be used in this lesson. Will you provide the data set or have students collect data? If the latter, what will be the sources of information they will use?

PHASE 2: EXAMINING AND ENUMERATING DATA

Data are easier to group if enumerated. Continuing with our example of plants, the teacher might place a numbered card under each plant so that students may discuss plants 1, 4, 7 and 14 as sharing a common attribute rather than by plant names (which students may not yet know).

Observer: did the teacher/students enumerate the data before attempting to categorize it?

Yes ☐   No ☐

PHASE 3: CLASSIFYING AND LABELLING DATA

Once a data set is assembled and enumerated and students have been instructed on procedures for grouping the data, the teacher will need to attend to the mechanics of the grouping activity. Students may work alone, in pairs, in small groups, or as one large group. Working alone requires the least social skill, and working in small groups the greatest social skill. If one objective is to develop students' abilities to work cooperatively, assertively defending their groupings but compromising when appropriate for group consensus, then students will need instruction and practice to develop these skills. If the teacher chooses to work with the entire class as a single group for the categorizing activity, he or she will need to exercise caution so that categories are not inadvertently provided for the students. Structuring students into pairs for the categorizing activity is the simplest way to have all students actively engaged in the task, although the teacher must again use considerable skill in keeping everyone involved while recording and synthesizing reports from the pairs. Teachers will probably want to experiment with different ways of structuring this activity, and pros and cons of each process can be discussed and problem-solved with peer coaches.

Teacher: please describe how you will organize students for the categorizing activity.

_____

_____

_____

Teacher: please describe how you will instruct the students to classify the data that you have provided or that they have collected.

_____

_____

_____

Observer: in your opinion, did the students understand the criteria and procedures they were to employ during the categorizing activity? Did the teacher inadvertently give clues about what the 'right' groups would be?

_____

_____

_____

_____

Observer: did the students work productively on the categorizing activity?

Yes ☐   No ☐   Partially ☐

If the teacher had the students work in pairs or small groups, did the students listen as other groups shared their categories?

Yes ☐   No ☐   Partially ☐

Were students able to explain the attributes on which they grouped items within categories?

Yes ☐   No ☐   Partially ☐

Were students able to provide names for their groups which reflected the attributes on which the groups were formed?

Yes ☐   No ☐

The names or labels students attach to groups of items within a data set will often accurately describe the group but not coincide with a technical or scientific name. For example, students may label a group of leaves 'jagged edges' while the technical term would be 'serrated edges'. The teacher may choose to provide technical or scientific terms when appropriate, but not before students have attempted to provide their own labels.

For some lessons, the content objectives will be accomplished at the conclusion of phase 3. When the teacher wishes to have students learn information by organizing it into categories and labelling it in order to gain conceptual control of the material, he or she may choose to stop here. Or when the objective is to learn what students see within a data set and what attributes they are unaware of, the grouping activity will accomplish that objective. When, however, the objective is the interpretation and application of concepts that have been formed in phase 3, the remainder of the inductive thinking model is appropriate. The final phases of the model result in further processing of the information and concepts embedded in the data set and should usually be completed.

PHASE 4: CREATING HYPOTHESES AND CONVERTING
CATEGORIES INTO SKILLS

One purpose of phase 4 is to help students develop understanding of possible relationships between and among categories that they have formed in phase 3. The class will need a common set of categories in order to work productively in this kind of discussion. Working off the descriptions of individual groups students have generated in phase 3, the teacher asks questions that focus students' thinking on similarities and differences between the groups. By asking 'why' questions, the teacher attempts to develop cause–effect relationships between the groups. The success of this phase depends on a thorough categorizing activity in phase 3, and the length of phase 4 is relatively short compared with the time required by phase 3.

Teacher: although you will not know during your planning what groups the students will form, make a guess about possible categories they might construct, and then write two sample questions that would explore cause–effect relationships between those groups.

_____

_____

_____

_____

Observer: were the students able to discuss possible cause–effect relationships among the groups?

Yes ☐   No ☐   Partially ☐

Did the teacher ask the students to go beyond the data and make inferences and conclusions regarding their data?

Yes ☐   No ☐

If yes, were the students able to do so?

Yes ☐   No ☐

If students were unable to make inferences or conclusions, can you think of any ideas to share with your partner that might help them do so?

_____

_____

_____

_____

If students were successful in making inferences and conclusions about their data, the teacher may wish to push them a step further and ask them to predict consequences from their data by asking 'What would happen if . . .' kinds of questions.

Teacher: please write one or two examples of hypothetical questions you might ask students about this data set.

_____

_____

_____

_____

Observer: were students able to make logical predictions based on the foregoing categorization and discussion?

Yes ☐   No ☐

Did the teacher ask the students to explain and support their predictions?

Yes ☐   No ☐

If students were unable to make logical predictions based on their previous work with their categories, can you think of questions or examples that might assist students in doing so?

_____

_____

_____

For teacher and observer discussion: are there writing assignments or other activities that would be appropriate extensions of this lesson?

COMMENTS ON STUDENT TRAINING NEEDS

In order to improve student performance, the first option we explore is whether it will improve with practice. That is, simple repetition of the model gives the students a chance to learn to respond more appropriately. Second, we directly teach the students the skills they need to manage the cognitive and social tasks of the model.

Observer: please comment on the skills with which the students engaged in the activities and suggest any areas where you believe training might be useful. Think especially of their ability to group by attributes, to provide labels for groups that accurately described the groups or synthesized attributes characteristic of a given group, their understanding of possible cause–effect relationships among groups, and their ability to make inferences or conclusions regarding their categories.

_____

_____

_____

_____

Teacher: how will you do this?

_____

_____

_____

_____

Observer: as the episode progressed, did the teacher gather information about whether the students were able to generate hypotheses?

Yes ☐   No ☐

Observer: were the students asked to compare the positives and contrast them with the negatives?

Yes ☐   No ☐

Learning to explore concepts

The guide is designed to assist peer coaching of the concept attainment model of learning and teaching. When planning questions, skip through the guide to the entries marked 'Teacher' and fill them in as needed. They will guide you through the model. Observers can use the guide to familiarize themselves with the plans of the teacher and to make notes about what is observed. Please remember, observers, that your primary function is not to give 'expert advice' to your colleague, but to observe the students as requested by the teacher and to observe the whole process so that you can gain ideas for your own teaching. The teacher is the coach in the sense that he or she is demonstrating a teaching episode for you. When you teach and are observed, you become the coach.

Teacher: do you want to suggest a focus for the analysis? If so, what is it?

_____

_____

THE TEACHING PROCESS

Most lessons have both content and process objectives. Content object-ives identify subject matter (facts, concepts, generalizations, relation-ships) to be mastered by students, while process objectives specify skills and procedures students need in order to achieve content objectives or auxiliary social objectives (for example, cooperation in a learning task).

Content objective

Teacher: please state the concept that is the objective of the lesson. What are its defining attributes? What kind of data will be presented to the students? Is the information or concept new to the students?

_____

_____

Process objective

Teacher: are the students familiar with the model? Do they need special assistance or training with respect to any aspect of the process?

_____

_____

Focus

The focus defines the field of search for the students. It may eliminate nonrelevant lines of inquiry. Often it is pitched at a level of abstraction just above the exemplars (i.e. 'a literary device' might serve as a focus for the concept of metaphor).

Teacher: please write the focus statement here.

_____

_____

Observer: did the teacher deliver the focus statement?

Yes ☐   No ☐

In your opinion, was it clear to the students and did it function to help them focus on the central content of the lesson?

Completely ☐   Partially ☐   No ☐

PHASE 1: PRESENTATION OF DATA AND IDENTIFICATION OF THE CONCEPT

The data set should be planned in pairs of positive and negative exemplars, ordered to enable the students – by comparing the positive exemplars and contrasting them with the negative ones – to distinguish the defining attributes of the concept.

Teacher: please describe the nature of the exemplars. (Are they words, phrases, documents, etc.? For example: 'These are reproductions of nineteenth-century paintings. Half of them are from the Impressionists [Renoir, Monet, Degas] and the other half are realistic, romantic or abstract paintings.')

_____

_____

The set

Observer: were approximately equal numbers of positive and negative exemplars presented?

Yes ☐   No ☐

Were the early positive exemplars clear and unambiguous?

Yes ☐   No ☐

Did the data set contain at least 15 each of positive and negative exemplars?

Yes ☐   No ☐

How was the set presented?
A labelled pair at a time?
All at once, with labels following?
Other (please describe)

_____

_____

Did the teacher provide the labels for the first eight or ten pairs
before asking the students to suggest a label?

Yes ☐   No ☐

PHASE 2: TESTING ATTAINMENT OF THE CONCEPT

As the students work through the data set, they are to examine each
exemplar and develop hypotheses about the concept. They need to ask
themselves what attributes the positive exemplars have in common. It is
those attributes that define the concept.
Teacher: how are you going to do this?

_____

_____

Observer: were the students asked to generate hypotheses but to
avoid sharing them?

Yes ☐   No ☐

Sometimes students are asked to record the progression of their
thinking.
Teacher: do you want to do this?

_____

_____

Observer: were the students asked to record their thinking as the
episode progressed?

Yes ☐   No ☐

As the lesson progresses, we need to get information about whether
the students are formulating and testing ideas.

PHASE 3: ANALYSIS OF THINKING STRATEGIES

When it appears that the students have developed hypotheses that they
are fairly sure of, they are asked to describe the progression of their
thinking and the concept they have arrived at.

Teacher: when to do this is a matter of judgement. How will you decide, and what will you say?

_____

_____

_____

Observer: did the teacher ask the students to share their thinking?

Yes ☐   No ☐

Were the students able to express their hypotheses?

Yes ☐   No ☐

If there were several hypotheses, could the students justify or reconcile them?

Yes ☐   No ☐

Naming and applying the concept

Once concepts have been agreed on (or different ones justified), they need names. After students have generated names, the teacher may need to supply the technical or common term (i.e. 'We call this style "Impressionism"'). Application requires that students determine whether further exemplars fit the concept and, perhaps, find examples of their own.

Teacher: is there a technical or common term the students need to know? How will you provide further experience with the concept?

_____

_____

_____

Observer: were the students able to name the concept?

Yes ☐   No ☐

Was a technical or common term for the concept supplied (if needed)?

Yes ☐   No ☐

Were additional exemplars provided?

Yes ☐   No ☐

Were the students asked to supply their own?

Yes ☐   No ☐

As the students examined new material, supplying their own exemplars, did they appear to know the concept?

Yes ☐   No ☐

An assignment to follow the lesson often involves the application of the concept to fresh material. For example, if the concept of *metaphor* had been introduced, the students might be asked to read a literary passage and identify the uses of metaphor in it.

Teacher: are you planning such an assignment? If so, please describe it briefly.

_____

_____

_____

COMMENTS ON STUDENT TRAINING NEEDS

In order to improve student performance, the first option we explore is whether it will improve with practice. That is, simple repetition of the model gives the students a chance to learn to respond more appropriately. Second, we directly teach the students the skills they need to manage the cognitive and social tasks of the model.

You might discuss:

How the students responded to phase I

Did they pay close attention to the focus statement and apply it to the examination of the exemplars? If not, is it worthwhile to give specific instruction and what might that be?

_____

_____

_____

How the students responded to phase 2

Did they compare and contrast the exemplars? Did they make hypotheses with the expectations that they might have to change them? Were they using the negative exemplars to eliminate alternatives? Is it worthwhile to provide specific training, and what might that be?

_____

_____

_____

How the students responded to phase 3

Were they able to debrief their thinking? Were they able to see how different lines of thinking gave similar or different results? Were they able to generate labels that express the concept? Do they understand how to seek exemplars on their own and apply what they have learned? Is it worthwhile to provide specific training, and what might that be?

_____

_____

_____

Learning to think metaphorically

The guide is designed to assist peer coaching of the synectics model of learning and teaching. When planning questions, skip through the guide to the entries marked 'Teacher' and fill them in as needed. They will guide you through the model. Observers can use the guide to familiarize themselves with the plans of the teacher and to make notes about what is observed. Please remember, observers, that your primary function is not to give 'expert advice' to your colleague, but to observe the students as requested by the teacher and to observe the whole process so that you can gain ideas for your own teaching. The teacher is the coach in the sense that he or she is demonstrating a teaching episode for you. When you teach and are observed, you become the coach.

Teacher: do you want to suggest a focus for the observer? If so, what is it?

_____

_____

THE TEACHING PROCESS

Most teaching episodes have both content and process objectives. Content objectives include the substance (information, concepts, generalizations, relationships, skills) to be mastered by students. Process objectives include skills or procedures the students need in order to learn productively from the cognitive and social tasks of the model.

Content objective(s)

Teacher: please state the content objectives of the episode. What kind of learning will come from the activity? What is the nature of the area to be explored?

_____

_____

_____

Process objective(s)

Teacher: are the students familiar with the model? Is there some aspect of its process where they need practice or instruction, and will you be concentrating on it in this lesson?

_____

_____

Observer: please comment on the students' response to the model. Do they appear to need specific help with some aspect of the process?

_____

_____

_____

PHASE 1: DESCRIPTION OF PRESENT CONDITION

Commonly synectics is used to generate fresh perspectives on a topic or problem either for clarification or to permit alternative conceptions or solutions to be explored. Thus it generally begins by soliciting from students a product representing their current thinking. They can formulate the problem, speak or write about the topic, enact a problem, draw a representation of a relationship – there are many alternatives. The function of this phase is to enable them to capture their current thoughts about the subject at hand.

Teacher: please describe how you will elicit the students' conceptions of the area to be explored. What will you say or do to orientate them?

_____

_____

_____

Observer: please comment on the students' response to the originating task. What is the nature of their conceptions?

_____

_____

_____

PHASES 2 AND 3: DIRECT AND PERSONAL ANALOGIES

The core of the model requires the development of distance from the original product through exercises inducing the students to make comparisons between sets of stimuli that are presented to them (direct analogy exercises) and to place themselves, symbolically, in the position of various persons, places and things (personal analogy exercises). The analogistic material generated in these exercises will be used later in the creation of further analogies called 'compressed conflicts'.

Teacher: what stimuli will you use to induce the students to make the direct and personal analogies? Please describe the material and the order in which you will proceed to stretch the students toward the more unusual and surprising comparisons.

_____

_____

_____

Observer: please comment on the stimuli and the student responses. Did the students get 'up in the air' metaphorically and generate less literal and more analogistic comparisons?

_____

_____

_____

PHASES 4 AND 5: COMPRESSED CONFLICT AND DIRECT ANALOGY

The next task is to induce the students to operate on the material generated in phases 2 and 3 and create compressed conflicts. You need to be prepared to define compressed conflict, even if the students have familiarity with the model, and to continue eliciting material until a number of examples clearly contain the logical (illogical?) tension that characterizes a high quality oxymoron.

Teacher: please describe how you will initiate phases 4 and 5 and how you will explain compressed conflict if you need to.

_____

_____

_____

_____

Observer: please comment on the student response to the task. How rich was the product?

_____

_____

_____

Now we ask the students to select some pairs that manifest great tension and to generate some analogies that represent the tension. For example, we might ask them to provide some examples of 'exquisite torture'.

Teacher: please describe briefly how you will present these tasks to the students.

_____

_____

_____

Observer: please discuss the students' understanding of the concept 'compressed conflict' and their ability to select the higher quality ones. Also, comment on the product of their attempt to generate oxymoronic analogies.

_____

_____

_____

_____

PHASE 6: RE-EXAMINATION OF THE ORIGINAL TASK

The compressed conflicts and the analogies to them provide material from which to revisit the original problem or topic. Sometimes we select or have the students select just one analogy with which to revisit the original material. At other times multiple perspectives are useful. What course to take depends on a combination of the complexity of the original problem or concept and the students' ability to handle new perspectives. For example, if a secondary social studies class has been trying to formulate potential solutions to a problem in international relations, we are dealing with a very complex problem for which multiple analogies are probably both appropriate and necessary. However, the task – helping the students share and assess a variety of analogies that can be used to redefine the problem and generate alternative solutions – is complex indeed.

Teacher: please describe how you will present the task of revisiting the original product. What will you ask the students to do?

_____

_____

_____

_____

Observer: please comment on the student products. What do you think has been the effect of the metaphoric exercises?

_____

_____

_____

_____

Now the new product needs to be examined. If the student worked as an individual or in a subgroup, the separate products need to be shared. If a problem is to be solved, new definitions and solutions need to be arranged. If written expression emerged, possibly it needs further editing. Unless the teaching episode is the conclusion of a topic of study, it generally leads to further study.

Teacher: please describe how the synectics products are to be shared and used. Will they lead to further reading and writing, data collection or experimentation?

_____

_____

_____

_____

Observer: please comment on the use of the new products. Are the students able to see the effects of the metaphoric activity? If they are asked to participate in further activities or to generate them, are they bringing to those tasks a 'set' toward the development of alternative perspectives or avenues?

_____

_____

_____

_____

COMMENTS ON STUDENT TRAINING NEEDS

It is the student who does the learning, and the greater the skill of the student in responding to the cognitive and social tasks of the model, the greater the learning is likely to be. Practice alone will build skill, and we want to provide plenty of it. After students are thoroughly familiar with the structure of the model, we can begin to develop specific training to improve their ability to perform.

Observer: please comment on the skills with which the students engaged in the activities and suggest any areas where you believe training might be useful. Think especially of their ability to make comparisons, their ability to take the roles required to make 'personal analogies', and their understanding of the structure of compressed conflicts and how to use them. Thinking back on the entire experience, is there any area where specific process training should be considered?

_____

_____

_____

_____

Learning mnemonically

During the last 15 years there has been renewed research and development on strategies for assisting students to master and retain information. The science of mnemonics, as it is called, has produced some
dramatic results (Pressley *et al.* 1981a, 1981b).

Rote repetition (rehearsing something over and over until it is
retained) has until recently been the primary method taught to students
for memorizing information and the primary method used by teachers
as they interact with students. In fact, rote methods have become so
used that they have become identified in many people's minds with the
act of memorization. To memorize, it is often thought, is to repeat by
rote.

MEMORIZATION STRATEGIES

However, although rehearsal of material continues to be one aspect of
most mnemonic strategies, a number of other procedures are employed
that greatly increase the probability that material will be learned and
retained. These procedures are combined in various ways, depending
on the material to be learned. Most of the procedures help build associations between the new material and familiar material. Some of the
procedures include:

Organizing information to be learned

The more information is organized the easier it is to learn and retain.
Information can be organized by categories. The concept-attainment,
inductive and advanced organizer models assist memory by helping
students associate the material in the categories. Consider the following
list of words from a popular spelling series, in the order the spelling
book presents them to the children:

soft	plus	cloth	frost	song
trust	luck	club	sock	pop
cost	lot	son	won	

Suppose we ask the children to classify them by beginnings, endings and
the presence of vowels. The act of classification requires the children to
scrutinize the words and associate words containing similar elements.
They can then name the categories in each classification (the *c* group and
the *st* group), calling further attention to the common attributes of the
group. They can also connect words that fit together (*pop song, soft cloth*,
etc.). They can then proceed to rehearse the spelling of one category at
a time. The same principle operates over other types of material – say,
number facts, etc. Whether categories are provided to students or
whether they create them, the purpose is the same. Also information
can be selected with categories in mind. The above list is, to outward
appearances, almost random. A list that deliberately and systematically

provides variations would be easier to organize (it would already have at least implicit categories within it).

Ordering information to be learned

Information learned in series, especially if there is meaning to the series, is easier to assimilate and retain. For example, if we wish to learn the names of the states of Australia it is easier if we always start with the same one (say, the largest) and proceed in the same order. Historical events by chronology are more easily learned than events sorted randomly. Order is simply another way of organizing information. We could have the students alphabetize their list of spelling words.

Linking information to familiar sounds

Suppose we are learning the names of the states. We can connect *Georgia* to *George*, *Louisiana* to *Louis*, *Maryland* to *Marry* or *Merry*, and so on. Categorizing the names of the states or ordering them by size, or ordering them within region, provides more associations.

Linking information to visual representations

Maryland can be linked to a picture of a marriage, Oregon to a picture of a gun, Maine to a burst water main, and so forth. Letters and numerals can be linked to something that evokes both familiar sounds and images. For example, *one* can be linked to *bun* and a picture of a boy eating a bun, *b* to *bee* and a picture of a bee. Those links can be used over and over again. 'April is the cruellest month, breeding lilacs out of the dead land' is easier remembered thinking of an ominous spring, bending malevolently over the spring flowers.

Linking information to associated information

A person's name, linked to information such as a well-known person having the same name, a soundalike, and some personal information, is easier to remember than the name rehearsed by itself. Louis (Louis Armstrong) 'looms' over Jacksonville (his place of birth). Learning the states of Australia while thinking of the points of the compass and the British origins of many of the names (New South Wales) is easier than learning them in order alone.

Making the information vivid

Devices that make the information vivid are also useful. Lorayne and Lucas favour 'ridiculous association', where information is linked to absurd associations. ('The silly two carries his twin two on his back so they are really four' and such.) Others favour the use of dramatization and vivid illustrations (such as counting the basketball players on two teams to illustrate that five and five equals ten).

Rehearsing

Rehearsal (practice) is always useful, and students benefit from knowledge of results. Students who have not had past success with tasks requiring memorization will benefit by having relatively short assignments and clear, timely feedback linked to their success.

PLANNING WITH MEMORIZATION IN MIND

The task of the teacher is to think up activities that help the students benefit from these principles.

A teaching episode or learning task that can be organized at least partly by these principles contains information to be learned. Both teacher and students should be clear that a very high degree of mastery is desired. (The students need to be trying to learn all the information and to retain it permanently.)

Teacher: please identify the information to be learned by your students in some curriculum area within a specified period of time.

_____

_____

_____

Which principles will you emphasize in order to facilitate memorization?

_____

_____

_____

Will these principles be used as the information is presented to the students? If yes, how?

_____

_____

_____

Which principles will be used as the students operate on the information? How?

_____

_____

_____

How will rehearsal and feedback be managed?

Observer: during the teaching/learning episode, situate yourself so that you can observe the behaviour of a small number of children (about a half dozen). Concentrate on their response to the tasks they are given.

Comment on their response. Do they appear to be clear about the objectives? Do they engage in the cognitive tasks that have been provided to them? Can they undertake these tasks successfully? Do they appear to be aware of progress?

DISCUSSION

The observer should report the results of the observation to the teacher. Then the discussion should focus on how the students responded and on ways of helping them respond more effectively, if that is desirable.

Practice frequently enables students to respond more productively without further instruction. Where instruction is needed, demonstration is useful. That is, the teacher may lead the students through the tasks over small amounts of material.

Tasks can be simplified in order to bring them within the reach of the students. We want the students to develop a repertoire of techniques that enable them to apply the mnemonic principles to learning tasks. Making the process conscious is a step toward independence, so we seek ways of helping the students understand the nature of the tasks and why these should work for them.

Learning through cooperative disciplined inquiry

Unlike the other guides in this series, this form to assist in the planning and observation of teaching is not built around a model of teaching. The substance is the organization of students into study groups and partnerships. It does not deal with the specific cooperative learning strategies developed by Robert Slavin and his associates (Slavin 1996) or Roger Johnson and David Johnson (1994), although the philosophy of the approach is similar. Nor does it deal specifically with group investigation (Thelen 1960; Sharan and Hertz-Lazarowitz 1980a, 1980b).

Rather, cooperative learning organization provides a setting for cooperative study that can be employed in combination with many approaches to teaching.

This guide describes some options and asks the teacher to select from them or to generate others. The observer analyses the students' productivity and attempts to identify ways of helping the students engage in more productive behaviour. The examples provided below are in reference to the inductive model of teaching. Using the two guides simultaneously may be useful.

When other models are being used, analogous use can be made of cooperative learning.

OPTIONS FOR ORGANIZATION

The underlying idea is to organize the students so that everyone in the class has a partner with whom they can work on instructional tasks. For example, pairs of students can operate throughout the inductive model, collecting information, developing categories and making inferences about causal relationships. The partnerships (which need not be long term, although they can be) are collected in teams. For example, if there are 30 students in the class, there can be five teams of six. We do not recommend teams larger than six. These teams can also work alongside the partnership structure. The partnerships provide an easy organization through which teams can divide labour. For example, each partnership can collect information from certain sources and then the information can be accumulated into a data set for the team. Similarly, team sets can be accumulated into a class set of data. Teams can then operate on these data sets and compare and contrast the results with those of other teams.

Team membership and partnerships can be organized in a number of ways, ranging from student selection, random selection, or teacher-guided choices to maximize heterogeneity and potential synergy.

Instruction of teams can range from explicit procedures to guide them through the learning activities to general procedures that leave much of the organization to the students.

Organization

Teacher: how will you organize the class for this teaching episode? How many groups of what sizes will be selected?

_____

_____

_____

_____

How will memberships be determined?

_____

_____

_____

_____

What approach to teaching/learning will be used? If you are not using a specific model of teaching, what will be your instructional strategy?

_____

_____

_____

_____

How will cooperative groups be used throughout the teaching episode? What cooperative tasks will be given to pairs, study groups or the whole class? For example, if this were an inductive lesson, partnerships might collect data, classify it and make inferences. Or partnerships might collect data, but it might be assembled by the entire class prior to the classification activity. Partnerships might study words, poems, maps, number facts and operations, or other material. What is your plan?

_____

_____

_____

_____

Observer: after you have familiarized yourself with the plan, situate yourself in the room so that you can observe about six students closely. Throughout the teaching episode, concentrate on the behaviour of those students, whether they are working in partnerships, study groups or any other organization. Then comment on their performance.

Did they appear to be clear about the tasks they were to accomplish? If not, can you identify what they were not clear about?

_____

_____

_____

_____

Did they appear to know how to cooperate to accomplish the tasks assigned to them? Is there anything they appear to need to know in order to be more productive?

_____

_____

_____

Do they regulate their own behaviour, keeping on task, dividing labour, taking turns? Could they profit from having any aspect of group management modelled for them?

_____

_____

_____

What sort of leadership patterns did they employ? Did they acknowledge one or more leaders? Did they discuss process? Were they respectful to one another?

_____

_____

_____

_____

Discussion

Following the episode, discuss the operation of the groups in which the six students were members. Is their productivity satisfactory? Their relationships? If not, see if you can develop a plan for helping the students become more productive. Remember that:

1 Providing practice is the simplest and most powerful way to help students learn to work productively. This is especially true if they have not had much experience working in cooperative groups.
2 The smaller the group, the more easily students can regulate their own behaviour. Reducing the size of study groups often allows students to solve their own problems.
3 Demonstration gets more mileage than exhortation. A teacher can join a group and show the students how to work together. In fact, the observer can be a participant in a study group in future sessions.
4 Simpler tasks are easier for students to manage. Breaking complex tasks into several smaller ones often allows students to build their skills through practice.
5 Praising appropriate behaviour gets results. If two groups are performing at different levels, it often helps to praise the productive group and then quietly join the less productive one and provide leadership.

Learning to study values

The guide is designed to assist peer coaching of the role playing model of learning and teaching. When planning questions, skip through the guide to the entries marked 'Teacher' and fill them in as needed. They will guide you through the model. Observers can use the guide to familiarize themselves with the plans of the teacher and to make notes about what is observed. Please remember, observers, that your primary function is not to give 'expert advice' to your colleague, but to observe the students as requested by the teacher and to observe the whole process so that you can gain ideas for your own teaching. The teacher is the coach in the sense that he or she is demonstrating a teaching episode for you. When you teach and are observed, you become the coach.

Teacher: do you want to suggest a focus for the analysis? If so, what is it?

_____

_____

THE TEACHING PROCESS

Most lessons have both content and process objectives. Content objectives identify subject matter (facts, concepts, generalizations, relationships) to be mastered by students, while process objectives specify skills and procedures students need in order to achieve content objectives or auxiliary social objectives (for example, cooperation in a learning task).

Content objective

Teacher: please state the objective of the lesson. What problem will be presented to the students, or in what domain will they construct a problem? Is the problem or domain of values new to the students?

_____

_____

Process objective

Teacher: are the students familiar with the model? Do they need special assistance or training with respect to any aspect of the process?

_____

_____

_____

PHASE 1: WARMING UP THE GROUP

Role playing begins with a social problem. The problem may be from a prepared study of a human-relations situation, or an aspect of human relations may be presented to the students so they can generate situations involving it. Possibly the problem is one in their lives that simply needs recapitulation.

Teacher: how will you present the problem to the students or help them develop it?

_____

_____

_____

Observer: in your opinion, was the problem clear to the students? Were they able to understand the nature of the problem and the type of human relationships problem it represents? Could they identify the players in the situation and how they act? Can they see the several sides of the problem?

_____

_____

_____

PHASE 2: SELECTING THE PARTICIPANTS (ROLE PLAYERS AND OBSERVERS)

Teacher: please describe how the participants will be selected.

_____

_____

_____

PHASE 3: SETTING THE STAGE

Teacher: how are you going to do this? Do you wish the first enactment to highlight certain aspects of values?

_____

_____

_____

Observer: were they able to generate a plausible and meaningful story line? Please note any difficulties they had.

_____

_____

_____

PHASE 4: PREPARING THE OBSERVERS

Once the characters have been identified and the story line generated, the observers (students) are prepared.

Teacher: what will you ask the observers to focus on?

_____

_____

_____

Sometimes the observers are asked to record the progression of their impressions.

Teacher: do you want to do this?

_____

_____

PHASE 5: THE ENACTMENT

Now the students enact the problem for the first time.

Observer: how well did the students enact the roles? Did they appear to empathize with the positions they were to take? Were the observers attentive and serious? Comment on any problems either role players or observers had.

_____

_____

_____

PHASE 6: DISCUSSION

Observer: were the students able to analyse the nature of the conflict and the values that were involved? Did they reveal their own value positions? Did they have any confusion about tactics of argumentation, skill and values?

_____

_____

_____

PHASES 7, 8 AND 9

From this point, phases 1 to 3 are repeated through several enactments. The teacher guides the students to ensure that the value questions are brought out.

Observer: please comment on the student performance in the ensuing cycles of enactments and discussions. Did the students increasingly become able to distinguish value positions?

_____

_____

_____

ANALYSIS

When the teacher judges that sufficient material has been generated, a discussion is held (a cooperative learning format can be used for this phase to maximize participation, if desired). This ensures that the value positions are brought out; the discussion also puts forward positions about what can be done to deal with the particular type of problem from a valuing basis rather than one involving adversarial uses of argumentation and conflict.

Teacher: please prepare the instructions you will give the students to inaugurate phase 4.

_____

_____

_____

Observer: please comment on the students' ability to handle the tasks involved in phase 4.

_____

_____

_____

DISCUSSION

Following the teaching episode, the coaching partners might discuss ways of helping the students respond more effectively to the model. Remember that the early trials are bound to be awkward and that practice often does the trick. Also problems can be adjusted to simplify the issues that have to be dealt with at any one time. Demonstrating the phases of the model to the students is also useful. The coaching partners can play the role of observer or even role player to give the students a model. Or the two teachers can demonstrate together.

Please summarize the results of the discussion – the one or two chief conclusions you have reached – to guide what you will next do as you use the model.

_____

_____

_____

_____

Learning through counselling

The guide is designed to assist peer coaching of the nondirective counselling model of learning and teaching. When planning questions, skip through the guide to the entries marked 'Teacher' and fill them in as needed. They will guide you through the model. Observers can use the guide to familiarize themselves with the plans of the teacher and to make notes about what is observed. Please remember, observers, that your primary function is not to give 'expert advice' to your colleague, but to observe the students as requested by the teacher and to observe the whole process so that you can gain ideas for your own teaching. The teacher is the coach in the sense that he or she is demonstrating a teaching episode for you. When you teach and are observed, you become the coach.

When first practising this model, we suggest that you work with individual students or very small groups

Teacher: do you want to suggest a focus for the observer? If so, what is it?

_____

_____

_____

THE TEACHING PROCESS

The most common use of the nondirective model is to help a student or a group of students (perhaps the entire class or even an entire student body) to understand their behaviour and take charge of some aspect of their development. The guide will focus on this type of use and will assume that the teaching episodes are to be built around helping the students approach an aspect of social development or an aspect of an academic area they are having trouble with. In other words, the guide assumes that you are contriving an encounter with the content to be studied.

Objectives

Teacher: please indicate the area of development you are focusing on during these episodes.

_____

_____

_____

_____

PHASES I AND 2: DEFINING THE HELPING SITUATION AND
EXPLORING THE PROBLEM

▄▄▄▄▄▄▄▄▄▄▄

Teacher: you need to open the discussion. How are you going to do this? Are you going to simply begin the discussion or are you going to set up an encounter with the area, such as showing a film, giving an assignment, asking the students to perform a task, or setting up a role playing enactment?

_____

_____

_____

Observer: how did the students respond? Did they appear to express themselves openly? For example, if the teacher is concentrating on students' anxiety in approaching problem solving in mathematics, was the anxiety expressed, albeit 'covered' by a rationale based on external causes?

_____

_____

_____

Observer: was the teacher able to reflect to the students on their expressions, and develop a preliminary picture of their conceptions, keeping individual differences in expression alive?

_____

_____

_____

PHASE 3: DEVELOPING INSIGHT

▄▄▄▄▄▄▄▄▄▄▄

Teacher: you need to figure out how you will induce the students to focus on an aspect of their behaviour and begin the process of accepting responsibility for changing themselves. How will you set up this aspect of the discussions?

_____

_____

_____

_____

Observer: please comment on the discussion. Were the students able to focus on some aspect of their behaviour? How did they handle the suggestion that they would have to make a change?

_____

_____

_____

PHASE 4: PLANNING AND DECISION MAKING

Teacher: you now need to induce the students to make a hypothesis that, if they change something, their situation will change. For example, if they have anxiety about some aspect of school work or some aspect of social interaction, they need to pick something they can do and practise doing it. How are you going to induce them to focus and develop their hypotheses?

_____

_____

_____

Observer: please indicate how the students responded. Do they have a course of action?

_____

_____

_____

PHASE 5: INTEGRATION

Now we work with the students to explore whether they are making progress. If their hypotheses aren't working, we help them develop new ones.

The phases are recycled as necessary. If Phase 3 breaks down, move back to Phase 1 or 2 and try again.

Observer: what do you think? Are the students making progress, both with the problem area and with their ability to respond to the tasks of the model?

_____

_____

Learning through simulations

The guide is designed to assist peer coaching of the simulation model of learning and teaching. When planning questions, skip through the guide to the entries marked 'Teacher' and fill them in as needed. They will guide you through the model. Observers can use the guide to familiarize themselves with the plans of the teacher and to make notes about what is observed. Please remember, observers, that your primary function is not to give 'expert advice' to your colleague, but to observe the students as requested by the teacher and to observe the whole process so that you can gain ideas for your own teaching. The teacher is the coach in the sense that he or she is demonstrating a teaching episode for you. When you teach and are observed, you become the coach.

Most simulations are embodied in print material or computer software. For most people, using such packaged simulations is the easiest way to begin the mastery of the model.

The structure of the guide assumes that students are just learning to use simulations and, therefore, pays attention to the process of teaching the students to use simulations.

Teacher: do you want to suggest a focus for the analysis? If so, what is it?

THE TEACHING PROCESS

Simulations provide tasks and feedback so that, by behaving and observing the results, the student can alter behaviour. The tasks and feedback cycles are arranged to help the students learn the structure of concepts in an area and the skills necessary for achieving particular objectives. Therefore, on completing a simulation exercise successfully, the students have acquired concepts and skills that need to be consolidated and brought under symbolic control. The students need to be able to articulate the concepts and describe the skills. In the best applications, they are asked to use them as they study other domains or areas of study.

Setting up the objectives requires that the teacher understands the simulation thoroughly. The teacher needs to engage in it personally in order to comprehend it fully.

Content objectives

Teacher: please describe the major concepts and skills that the students are to learn.

_____

_____

_____

_____

Process objectives

Teacher: are the students familiar with the process of the model? Do they need special help with any aspect of the process?

_____

_____

_____

_____

PHASE I: ORIENTATION

The students need to know the kind of objectives they are to achieve with the particular simulation. One does not tell them the specific objectives and skills they will learn, but rather the kinds of concepts and skills they will learn.

Teacher: how will you do this? What major points will you emphasize?

_____

_____

_____

Observer: do you think the students understand the kinds of things they are to learn?

_____

_____

_____

_____

PHASE 2: PARTICIPANT TRAINING

This phase may take several sessions. The teacher's role is to help the students get going and to help them solve problems.

Teacher: what kinds of help do you anticipate having to provide?

_____

_____

_____

_____

Observer: did the students appear able to take on the tasks? How did they respond to feedback? Do they appear to understand what they are to learn?

_____

_____

_____

_____

PHASE 3: SIMULATION OPERATIONS

In this phase, the students reach the end of a segment of the simulation or the entire simulation. They need to reflect on what they have learned – what worked and didn't work – and establish conscious control over the concepts and skills.

Teacher: how will you conduct this session or these sessions? What will you ask the students? How will the information be recorded?

_____

_____

_____

_____

Observer: how effectively were the students able to articulate the concepts and skills essential to successful performance?

_____

_____

_____

PHASE 4: PARTICIPANT DEBRIEFING

We suggest that the students write about the area they have studied or develop written/oral presentations, including graphics, that describe the learning.

Teacher: please describe the task you will give the students and how the products of the task will be shared.

_____

_____

_____

_____

Observer: did the students understand the task? Did they engage in it knowledgeably? What further help do they need to consolidate their learning?

_____

_____

_____

_____

COMMENTARY

These phases can be recycled and repeated as necessary. A long simulation may require several revisitations of various phases and may actually be conducted as a series of segments that include all the phases.

References

Applebee, A., Langer, J., Jenkins, L., Mullis, I. and Foertsch, M. (1990) *Learning to Write in our Nation's Schools*. Washington, DC: US Department of Education.

Aronson, E., Blaney, N., Stephan, C., Sikes, J. and Snapp, M. (1978) *The Jigsaw Classroom*. Beverly Hills, CA: Sage.

Atkinson, J. W. (1966) *Achievement Motivation*. New York: John Wiley and Sons.

Ball, S. and Bogatz, G. A. (1970) *The First Year of Sesame Street*. Princeton, NJ: Educational Testing Service.

Baveja, B. (1988) An exploratory study of the use of information-processing models of teaching in secondary school biology science classes. Ph.D. thesis, Delhi, India: Delhi University.

Baveja, B., Showers, B. and Joyce, B. (1985) *An Experiment in Conceptually-based Teaching Strategies*. Eugene, OR: Booksend Laboratories.

Becker, W. and Gersten, R. (1982) A followup of Follow Through: the later effects of the direct instruction model on children in the fifth and sixth grades, *American Educational Research Journal*, 19(1): 75–92.

Bloom, B. S. (1984) The 2 sigma problem: the search for group instruction as effective as one-to-one tutoring, *Educational Researcher*, 13: 4–16.

Boocock, S. S. and Schild, E. (1968) *Simulation Games in Learning*. Beverly Hills, CA: Sage Publications.

Bredderman, T. (1983) Effects of activity-based elementary science on student outcomes: a quantitative synthesis, *Review of Educational Research*, 53(4): 499–518.

Bruner, J. (1961) *The Process of Education*. Cambridge, MA: Harvard University Press.

Bruner, J. (1966) *Toward a Theory of Instruction*. Cambridge, MA: Harvard University Press.

Bruner, J., Goodnow, J. J. and Austin, G. A. (1967) *A Study of Thinking*. New York: Science Editions.

Central Advisory Council for Education (England) (1967) *Children and their Primary Schools* (Plowden Report). London: HMSO.

Chamberlin, C. and Chamberlin, E. (1943) *Did They Succeed in College?* New York: Harper and Row.

Chesler, M. and Fox, R. (1966) *Role-playing Methods in the Classroom*. Chicago: Science Research Associates.

Dewey, J. (1916) *Democracy in Education*. New York: Macmillan.

Downey, L. (1967) *The Secondary Phase of Education*. Boston, MA: Ginn.

Edmunds, R. (1979) Effective schools for the urban poor, *Educational Leadership*, 37(1): 15–27.

El-Nemr, M. A. (1979) Meta-analysis of the outcomes of teaching biology as inquiry. Unpublished doctoral dissertation, Boulder: University of Colorado.

Estes, W. E. (ed.) (1976) *Handbook of Learning and Cognitive Processes, Vol. IV: Attention and Memory*. Hillsdale, NJ: Lawrence Erlbaum Associates.

Gagné, R. (1965) *The Conditions of Learning*. New York: Holt, Rinehart and Winston.

Gerbner, G. (1974) Teacher images in mass culture: symbolic functions of the 'hidden curriculum', in *Media and Symbols*, the seventy-third yearbook of the National Society for the Study of Education. Chicago: University of Chicago Press.

Glass, G. V. (1982) Meta-analysis: an approach to the synthesis of research results, *Journal of Research in Science Teaching*, 19(2): 93–112.

Glynn, S. M. (1994) *Teaching Science with Analogies*. Athens, GA: National Reading Research Center, University of Georgia.

Goffman, I. (1982) *Gender Advertisements*. New York: Harper and Row.

Goodlad, J. and Klein, F. (1970) *Looking behind the Classroom Door*. Worthington, OH: Charles A. Jones.

Gordon, W. J. J. (1961) *Synectics*. New York: Harper and Row.

Gordon, W. J. J. (1970) The metaphorical development of man, in C. Brooks (ed.) *The Changing World and Man*. New York: New York University Press.

Gordon, W. J. J. (1971) Architecture – the making of metaphors, *Main Currents in Modern Thought*, 28(1).

Guetzkow, H., *et al.* (1963) *Simulation in International Relations*. Englewood Cliffs, NJ: Prentice-Hall.

Hillocks, G. (1987) Synthesis of research on teaching writing, *Educational Leadership*, 44(8): 71–82.

Hopkins, D. (1987) *Knowledge, Information Skills and the Curriculum*. London: British Library.

Hopkins, D. (in press) *Theories of Development, Strategies for Growth. Tensions in and Prospects for School Improvement* (International Handbook on Education: Volume IV). Dordrecht, The Netherlands: Kluwer Academic.

Hopkins, D., Ainscow, M. and West, M. (1994) *School Improvement in an Era of Change*. London: Cassell.

Hopkins, D., West, M. and Ainscow, M. (1996) *Improving the Quality of Education for All*. London: David Fulton.

Hunt, D. E. (1971) *Matching Models in Education*. Toronto: Ontario Institute for Studies in Education.

Hunter, I. M. L. (1964) *Memory*. London: Penguin.

Johnson, D. W. and Johnson, R. T. (1974) Instructional goal structure: cooperative, competitive, or individualistic, *Review of Educational Research*, 44: 213–40.

Johnson, D. W. and Johnson, R. T. (1981) Effects of cooperative and individualistic learning experiences on inter-ethnic interaction, *Journal of Educational Psychology*, 73(3): 444–9.

Johnson, D. W. and Johnson, R. T. (1990) *Cooperation and Competition: Theory and Research*. Edina, MN: Interaction Book Company.

Johnson, D. W. and Johnson, R. T. (1993) *Circles of Learning*. Englewood Cliffs, NJ: Prentice-Hall.

Johnson, D. W. and Johnson, R. T. (1994) *Learning Together and Alone*. Englewood Cliffs, NJ: Prentice-Hall.

Joyce, B. (1991) Common misconceptions about cooperative learning and gifted students, *Educational Leadership*, 48(6): 72–4.

Joyce, B. and Calhoun, E. (eds) (1996) *Learning Experiences in School Renewal*. Eugene, OR: ERIC Clearinghouse.

Joyce, B. and Showers, B. (1983) *Power in Staff Development through Research on Training*. Washington, DC: Association for Supervision and Curriculum Development.

Joyce, B. and Showers, B. (1995) *Student Achievement through Staff Development*, 2nd edn. White Plains, NY: Longman.

Joyce, B. and Weil, M. (1975) *Models of Teaching*. Englewood Cliffs, NJ: Prentice-Hall.

Joyce, B. and Weil, M. (1996) *Models of Teaching*, 5th edn. Englewood Cliffs, NJ: Prentice-Hall.

Joyce, B., Showers, B., Murphy, C. and Murphy, J. (1989) Reconstructing the workplace: school renewal as cultural change, *Educational Leadership*, 47(3): 70–8.

Joyce, B., Calhoun, E., Halliburton, C., Simser, J., Rust, D. and Carran, N. (1994) The Ames Community Schools staff development program. Paper presented at the annual meeting of the Association for Supervision and Curriculum Development, Chicago.

Joyce, B., Calhoun, E., Halliburton, C., Simser, J., Rust, D. and Carran, N. (1996) University town, in B. Joyce and E. Calhoun (eds) *Learning Experiences in School Renewal*. Eugene, OR: ERIC Clearinghouse.

Kagan, S. (1990) *Cooperative Learning Resources for Teachers*. San Juan Capistrano, CA: Resources for Teachers.

Kohlberg, L. (1981) *The Philosophy of Moral Development*. New York: Harper and Row.

Levin, M. E. and Levin, J. R. (1990) Scientific mnemonics: methods for maximizing more than memory, *American Educational Research Journal*, 27: 301–21.

Levine, D. Y. and Lezotte, L. W. (1990) *Unusually Effective Schools: A Review and Analysis of Research and Practice*. Madison, WI: The National Center for Effective Schools Research and Development.

Lorayne, H. and Lucas, J. (1966) *The Memory Book*. New York: Briercliff Manor.

MacGilchrist, B., Mortimer, P., Savage, J. and Beresford, C. (1995) *Planning Matters*. London: Paul Chapman.

McKinney, C., Warren, A., Larkins, G., Ford, M. J. and Davis, J. C. III (1983) The effectiveness of three methods of teaching social studies concepts to fourth-grade students: an aptitude-treatment interaction study, *American Educational Research Journal*, 20: 663–70.

Mortimore, P., Sammons, P., Stoll, L., Lewis, D. and Ecols, R. (1988) *School Matters*. London: Open Books.

Newby, T. J. and Ertner, P. A. (1994) Instructional analogies and the learning of concepts. A paper delivered to the annual meeting of the American Educational Research Association, New Orleans.

Oakes, J. (1986) *Keeping Track: How Schools Structure Inequality*. New Haven, CT: Yale University Press.

Pinnell, G. S. (1989) Helping at-risk children learn to read, *Elementary School Journal*, 90(2): 161–84.

Pressley, M. (1977) Children's use of the keyword method to learn simple Spanish vocabulary words, *Journal of Educational Psychology*, 69(5): 465–72.

Pressley, M. and Dennis-Rounds, J. (1980) Transfer of a mnemonic keyword strategy at two age levels, *Journal of Educational Psychology*, 72(4): 575–82.

Pressley, M., Levin, J. and Miller, G. (1981a) How does the keyword method affect vocabulary, comprehension, and usage? *Reading Research Quarterly*, 16: 213–26.

Pressley, M., Levin, J. and Miller, G. (1981b) The keyword method and children's learning of foreign vocabulary with abstract meanings, *Canadian Psychology*, 35(3): 283–7.

Pressley, M., Levin, J. R. and Delaney, H. D. (1982) The mnemonic keyword method, *Review of Educational Research*, 52(1): 61–91.

Qin, Z., Johnson, D. W. and Johnson, R. T. (1995) Cooperative versus competitive efforts and problem solving, *Review of Educational Research*, 65(2).

Quellmatz, E. S. and Burry, J. (1983) *Analytic Scales for Assessing Students' Expository and Narrative Writing Skills*, CSE Resource Paper No. 5. Los Angeles: Center for the Study of Evaluation, UCLA Graduate School of Education.

Roebuck, F., Buhler, J. and Aspy, D. (1976) A comparison of high and low levels of humane teaching/learning conditions on the subsequent achievement of students identified as having learning difficulties. Final report: Order No. PLD 6816–76 re. the National Institute of Mental Health. Denton, TX: Texas Woman's University Press.

Rogers, C. (1961) *On Becoming a Person*. Boston, MA: Houghton Mifflin.

Rogers, C. (1982) *Freedom to Learn for the Eighties*. Columbus, OH: Charles E. Merrill.

Rudduck, J. and Hopkins, D. (eds) (1985) *Research as a Basis for Teaching: Readings from the Work of Lawrence Stenhouse*. London: Heinemann.

Rutter, M., Maughan, B., Mortimer, P. and Ouston, J. (1979) *Fifteen Thousand Hours*. London: Open Books.

Sanders, D. A. and Sanders, J. A. (1984) *Teaching Creativity through Metaphor*. New York: Longman.

Sarason, S. (1982) *The Culture of the School and the Problem of Change*, 2nd edn. Boston, MA: Allyn and Bacon.

Shaftel, F. and Shaftel, G. (1967) *Role Playing of Social Values: Decision Making in the Social Studies*. Englewood Cliffs, NJ: Prentice-Hall.

Shaftel, F. and Shaftel, G. (1982) *Role Playing in the Curriculum*. Englewood Cliffs, NJ: Prentice-Hall.

Sharan, S. (1980) Cooperative learning in small groups: recent methods and effects on achievement, attitudes, and ethnic relations, *Review of Educational Research*, 50(2): 241–71.

Sharan, S. (1990) *Cooperative Learning: Theory and Research*. New York: Praeger.

Sharan, S. and Hertz-Lazarowitz, R. (1980a) Academic achievement of elementary school children in small group versus whole-class instruction, *Journal of Experimental Education*, 48(2): 120–9.

Sharan, S. and Hertz-Lazarowitz, R. (1980b) A group investigation method of cooperative learning in the classroom, in S. Sharan, P. Hare, C. Webb and R. Hertz-Lazarowitz (eds) *Cooperation in Education* (pp. 14–46). Provo, UT: Brigham Young University Press.

Sharan, S. and Shachar, H. (1988) *Language and Learning in the Cooperative Classroom*. New York: Springer-Verlag.

Skinner, B. F. (1953) *Science and Human Behavior*. New York: Macmillan.

Slavin, R. E. (1983) *Cooperative Learning*. New York: Longman.

Slavin, R. E. (1990) Achievement effects of ability grouping in secondary schools, *Review of Educational Research*, 60(3): 471–500.

Slavin, R. E. (1991) Are cooperative learning and 'untracking' harmful to the gifted? *Educational Leadership*, 48(6): 68–70.

Slavin, R. E. (1996) *Education for All*. Lisse, The Netherlands: Swets and Zertlinger.

Slavin, R. E., Madden, N. A., Karweit, N., Livermon, B. J. and Dolan, L. (1990) Success for all: first-year outcomes of a comprehensive plan for reforming urban education. *American Educational Research Journal*, 27: 255–78.

Smith, K. and Smith, M. (1966) *Cybernetic Principles of Learning and Educational Design*. New York: Holt, Rinehart and Winston.

Smith, M. L. (1980) *Effects of Aesthetics Education on Basic Skills Learning*. Boulder, CO: Laboratory of Educational Research, University of Colorado.

Spaulding, R. (1970) *Early Intervention Program*. Durham, NC: Duke University Press.

Stenhouse, L. (1975) *An Introduction to Curriculum Research and Development*. London: Heinemann.

Stenhouse, L. (ed.) (1980) *Curriculum Research and Development in Action*. London: Heinemann.

Taba, H. (1966) *Teaching Strategies and Cognitive Functioning in Elementary School Children* (Cooperative Research Project 2404). San Francisco: San Francisco State College.

Taba, H. (1967) *Teachers' Handbook for Elementary School Social Studies*. Reading, MA: Addison-Wesley.

Tennyson, R. D. and Cocchiarella, M. (1986) An empirically based instructional design theory for teaching concepts, *Review of Educational Research*, 56: 40–71.

Thelen, H. (1954) *Dynamics of Groups at Work*. Chicago: University of Chicago Press.

Thelen, H. (1960) *Education and the Human Quest*. New York: Harper and Row.

Thelen, H. (1967) *Classroom Grouping for Teachability*. New York: John Wiley and Sons.

White, W. A. T. (1986) The effects of direct instruction in special education: a meta-analysis. Ph.D. thesis, University of Oregon.

Wolpe, J. and Lazarus, A. (1966) *Behavior Therapy Techniques: A Guide to the Treatment of Neuroses*. Oxford: Pergamon Press.

Index

CHANGING OUR SCHOOLS
LINKING SCHOOL EFFECTIVENESS AND SCHOOL
IMPROVEMENT

Louise Stoll and Dean Fink

Many of our schools are good schools – if this were 1965. Processes and structures designed for a time that has passed are no longer appropriate in a rapidly changing society. Throughout the world a great deal of effort and money has been expended in the name of educational change. Much of it has been misdirected and some of it wasteful. This book assists people inside and outside schools to bring about positive change by helping them to define the purposes behind change, the processes needed to achieve change and the results which they should expect. By linking the *why*, *what* and *how* of change, the authors provide both a theoretical critique and practical advice to assist all those committed to changing and improving schools.

> Very few books on school reform contain so many ideas and insights while managing to construct a coherent and comprehensive message. Stoll and Fink have written an invaluable resource which is rich both conceptually and practically. This is a book that can be read in part or whole with great profit.
>
> Michael Fullan

Contents

Good schools if this were 1965: the context of change – The Halton Effective Schools Project: a story of change – School effectiveness can inform school improvement – The possibilities and challenges of school improvement – School development planning: a path to change – The power of school culture – Invitational leadership – Changing the concepts of teaching and learning – The need for partnerships – Learning for all: building the learning community – Evaluate what you value – Changing our schools: linking school effectiveness and school improvement – References – Index.

240pp   0 335 19290 4 (paperback)   0 335 19291 2 (hardback)

A TEACHER'S GUIDE TO CLASSROOM RESEARCH (SECOND EDITION)

David Hopkins

A Teacher's Guide to Classroom Research is a practical guide for teachers who wish to undertake research in their classrooms and schools for the purpose of improving practice. Classroom research, as described in this book, enables teachers to enhance their own or a colleague's teaching, to test the assumptions of educational theory in practice, and to implement and evaluate whole school developments.

The educational landscape in Britain has changed dramatically since this book was originally published in 1985. The increase in centralized policy making, however, far from undermining the role of the 'teacher researcher', has made such a professional ethic all the more necessary. Teacher researchers now have to interpret and adapt policy to their own teaching situation and to link their classroom research work to that of other colleagues and whole school priorities.

The second edition of *A Teacher's Guide to Classroom Research* takes this new perspective into account whilst retaining the structure and simplicity of the original book. In particular, the crucial role of classroom observation in supporting teacher and school development is emphasized, a new chapter on linking classroom research to other whole school initiatives has been added, and the text as a whole has been updated in light of the changing context.

Contents

A teacher's guide to classroom research − Classroom research in action − Why classroom research by teachers? − Action research and classroom research by teachers − Developing a focus − Principles of classroom observation − Methods of observation in classroom research − Data gathering − Analysing classroom research data − Maintaining the action − Classroom research and school improvement − Seeing teacher development whole − Appendix: ethics for classroom research − References − Name index − Subject index.

256pp   0 335 19065 0 (paperback)